Dave Pelz's Damage Control

Also by Dave Pelz: Putt Like the Pros
Dave Pelz's Short Game Bible
Dave Pelz's Putting Bible
Dave Pelz's 10 Minutes a Day to Better Putting

Published by the Pelz Golf Institute,

The Pelz Golf Institute
20308 Hwy 71W
Spicewood, TX 78669
800-833-7370 www.pelzgolf.com

Photo Credits on page 306

ISBN: 0-9778138-0-0
Library of Congress Catalog Number: 2006902237

Printed in the United States of America
April 2006
First Edition

10 09 08 07 06 1 2 3 4 5 6 7 8 9 10

Damage Control is a trademark of Pelz Golf

Dave Pelz's
Damage Control

Dave Pelz
with Eddie Pelz
& Joel Mendelman

Dedication

I dedicate this book to our future golfers. Of course, I hope Damage Control will help older golfers (like you and me) play with fewer disasters, lower our handicaps, and realize our scoring potential.

More importantly, however, I dedicate this book to our upcoming generations of future golfers, in the hope they will develop and use Damage Control to minimize their disaster scoring ... by NOT working on their games only from perfect lies on flat practice tees, like the rest of us have done.

In this regard, I encourage all "disaster-hole-inflicted" parents to get out in your backyards and play with Damage Control balls and techniques with your kids. Play games hitting shots from crazy lies off sloped platforms, mounds, under trees, off trays of water and mats with sand. As you learn the concepts of Damage Control, you'll expose them to a veritable palate of swings, ideas and techniques, early in their golf careers. And it could be invaluable to their games.

So share and enjoy Damage Control with your kids and grand kids. It's fun, beneficial to all, and good for the game of golf. Because no one enjoys making disaster scores on a hole and no one needs to any more!

Contents

Set-up-ology is the study of how to set-up for trouble shots. A golfer's set-up can enable … or prohibit … the success of any escape attempt from trouble.

When your normal swing won't get you out of trouble … create an escape swing that will!

When extra force is needed to power clubs through water, sand, bushes or grass, turning up your hand-fire is the answer.

Acknowledgements

The authors would like to acknowledge and express special appreciation to the many people and facilities that have helped us so much in learning about Damage Control.

In particular we thank Tim Blixseth of Porcupine Creek (Palm Springs), Brady Omen of Escondido Country Club (Horse Shoe Bay), Director of Golf Glen Lee of the Hills of Lakeway (Austin), and the Legends Resorts (Myrtle Beach) for your kindness and hospitality, and giving us access to superb facilities. The photographs in this book do not do justice to the incredible beauty we encountered while demonstrating the fundamentals of Damage Control at your courses.

We also want to thank Leonard Kamsler, the world's best golf photographer, and our good friends at Golf Magazine and the Golf Channel for their help in photographing and recording the players, conditions and circumstances of Damage Control.

Thanks also go to our friends at Myrtle Beach Golf Holiday, DuPont, the PGA Tour Superstore, and the amateur contestants in the World Handicap Amateur Championships in Myrtle Beach South Carolina, who allowed us and helped us to perform the research which forms the basis of this book.

We sincerely appreciate the help Sven Nilson provided in graphical presentations for this book and the many and varied roundtable discussions of the entire Pelz Golf Institute staff, especially Tom Sieckmann, for his demonstrations and insights on Damage Control from the point of view of a PGA Tour champion. We also send a thank you to Pete Piotrowski for his help in the organization and analysis of some of our Institute data.

We thank the PGA Tour players who demonstrated their skills and communicated their thoughts honestly and straightforwardly to us along the way. Without being able to watch you (Phil, Vijay, Payne, Lee, Elk and Mike) up close and study how you escape from trouble, the five skills of Damage Control may never have been recognized and this book certainly would never have been written.

And finally, we thank those particular players in the World Amateur who tried their best - no matter what kind of trouble-mess they found themselves in - but came up making disaster scores on disaster holes. Your efforts and consternation led us to the problem in the first place, and gave us the last four years of pure enjoyment in figuring out the answer.

Golf is important to me. I've played it for more than 50 years, studied it for 40, conducted research on it for 35, and taught it professionally for 30. Just recently, however, I've learned something new … and very important … about the game. In a research project at the Pelz Golf Institute involving thousands of golfers, I learned:

> - Golfers play two to five strokes below their handicap for most of each round.
> - In most rounds they also play badly (above their handicap) on a few "disaster" holes, bringing their scores back up to handicap level
> - There is a way to avoid these disaster scores, and lower golfers' handicaps

Working with my staff at the Institute, we've developed the fix for disaster scores. We call it Damage Control.™

Question #1: What's the Problem?

Answer #1: *Disaster scores and disaster holes are the problem.*

Think about your game. You play well most of the time, but always seem to mess up a few holes that ruin your score. This doesn't happen once or twice a year. You do it consistently, almost like an unwritten law: "You can't put together a complete 18-hole round without a disaster score or two". It happens to most golfers. It's the way the game is played!

Here are some facts about the way you play. You:

> - play well (below your handicap) for most of each round (14 to 17 holes).
> - have a few "disaster" holes, with seriously high scores.
> - are disappointed with your score and know you are capable of playing better.
> - blame your disaster holes on errant shots which get into trouble.
> - believe you must practice more and improve your swing to avoid trouble, and eliminate disaster scores.

And some generic facts about the game:

> - Golfers get away with most of their errant shots, which are actually part of their normal game.
> - Errant shots usually don't cause disaster scores, but they do present opportunities for them.
> - Disaster scores usually occur after a failed recovery attempt (the shot played **after** an errant shot) flys out of trouble … into even worse trouble (out of the frying pan … into the fire).

Question #2: What's the Answer?

Answer #2: *Damage Control is the answer.*

Recovery shots from trouble often fail because golfers don't know how to swing from weird stances on uneven terrain, with a bush behind the ball, and a tree limb in the way. They try to escape using normal swings which don't work from trouble. They also aim at inappropriate targets, without realizing it. These problems can be eliminated by Damage Control, which enables golfers to escape trouble without ruining their score!

Some facts about trouble:

> - Golfers will never completely avoid errant shots (they're human).
> - Courses are designed to make sure you get into trouble. You will get into it. You'd better learn to deal with it.
> - Even if you don't hit bad shots, bad luck and bad bounces will get you into trouble. That's golf.
> - Even the world's best players hit errant shots into trouble. It's part of the game; always has been, always will be.
> - Once you learn Damage Control, getting into trouble need no longer routinely ruin your game.
> - **Damage Control requires skills different from those normally practiced and used from good lies.**

Question #3: What's the effect of Damage Control?

Answer #3: : *It limits damage to less than one stroke- when you get into serious trouble.*

Damage Control is a skill you can develop in golf, like long-driving and lag-putting. Good long-drivers hit drives a long way and in the fairway a good percentage of the time. Good lag-putters don't three-putt often. And good Damage Control players limit the damage to less than one stroke when they get into trouble.

Damage Control is:

> - escaping from trouble first … recovering from trouble second.
> - escaping into a better position than you would have been in … had your previous shot not gotten into trouble.
> - escaping from trouble on the first try.
> - recovering … after escape from trouble … with less than one stroke lost to your score.

Question #4: What is Damage Control?

Answer #4: *Damage Control combines five skills to eliminate disaster scores from your game.*

The five skills of Damage Control are:

- Set-up-ology (Chapter #2): How to set-up for trouble swings
- Swing Shaping (Chapter #3): How to execute escape swings which differ from the norm
- Hand-Fire Feel (Chapter #4): How to use your hands in escape shots
- Red-Flag Touch (Chapter #5): How to plan for the behavior of trouble shots after they are launched
- Damage Control Mentality (Chapter #6): How to use the Damage Controller

Question #5: Who Needs Damage Control?

Answer #5: : *We all … all golfers … need damage control in our games, because "Golf … as Life … is full of unforced errors".*

Golf deals us bad breaks and bad bounces all the time … sometimes even after we've performed well.

> - The higher your handicap and the more trouble you get into, the more strokes Damage Control can save you.
> - The skills of Damage Control are unrecognized, unpracticed, and completely missing from most golfers' games.
> - Damage Control can not be learned in normal practice on normal ranges with flat practice tees.

Question #6: Why haven't you heard about Damage Control before now?

Answer #6: *Because it's new!*

I played my entire career trying to get good enough to stay out of trouble while never practicing getting-out of trouble, which is what I actually needed.

I only recently became aware of how amateurs consistently screw up their scores with disaster holes. At the same time I've been coaching two of the world's best players, Phil Mickelson and Vijay Singh, seeing how they save their scores after their errant shots find trouble. In putting these two efforts together, I discovered why amateurs score disastrously from trouble while pros don't. I recognized five skills pros have that amateurs don't have. These are the five skills of Damage Control.

Damage Control will work for you, if you:

- Step #1: Read this entire book
- Step #2: Practice Damage Control swings at home in your backyard
- Step #3: Play a few "Damage Control" practice rounds at your local course
- Step #4: Make the emotional commitment to play with Damage Control.

I promise … it will be worth the effort. Damage Control will help you shoot lower scores!

Damage Control is not about making perfect golf swings, improving the swing you have, or how to stay out of trouble in the first place. Damage Control is getting out of trouble, without ruining your score.

Research at the Pelz Golf Institute shows golfers get into trouble in almost every round … and they're not really good at getting out of it. A few times each round they play shots from trouble into worse trouble (out of the frying pan … into the fire), and make disastrous scores on what we call "disaster holes."

Golf, like life, is full of unforced errors. To combat its troubles, Dave Pelz's Damage Control has been developed from the scientific analysis of golfers' on-course performance, which shows five skills are missing in most amateur's ability to play from difficult lies. Learning these skills, and avoiding disaster holes, is what Dave Pelz's Damage Control is all about.

1.1 The Big Picture

Golf is the greatest game. It's the game of a lifetime, a game of honor, a game for all ages. It can't be bought; it plays no favorites and provides a well known condition: the better you play, the lower you score ... the more fun you have.

The goal of my working life is to understand golf well enough, and teach it simply enough, to help golfers score better and have more fun. In pursuit of this goal, research first led me to putting, then to the short game, and now to Damage Control. The purpose of this book is to show you our new concept of Damage Control, and how it can lower your scores 2 to 5 shots per round. And please make no mistake: Damage Control can do exactly that!

To help you understand Damage Control, we will first step back and look at a big picture of the game (it's often beneficial to see the big picture ... before trying to understand the details of a problem). This means taking a few moments to look at the big picture of golf ... how it is played ... why things happen in the game ... before trying to learn how Damage Control fits into it.

1.1.1 The cycle of golf

Golf is played one shot at a time, the fewer ... the better. We start at the first hole hitting and chasing the ball repeatedly, until we hole-out on the last hole. Then, we add up our score and smile, frown, or feel something in-between. Research based on tournament score cards (covering a wide range of skill levels) shows most golfers play reasonably well on most holes, but then waste several shots on a few trouble holes somewhere during each round. To understand this, let's look into the very core of the game ... the fundamental cycle of golf.

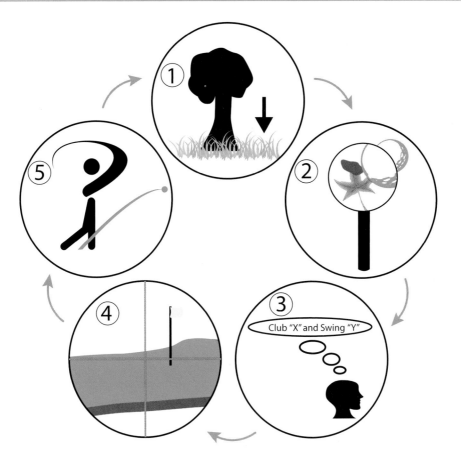

Club "X" and Swing "Y"

1.1.1.1

The essence of the game can be netted-out in one cycle (shot). In each cycle, (Figure 1.1.1.1) the golfer must first 1) find the ball, whether it's in his bag before the round starts, in his pocket between holes, or somewhere on the course in play. After the ball is found, 2) its lie or condition of play is evaluated (including materials around the ball, stance requirements and any obstacles to the upcoming swing which may be involved). Then, 3) the golfer selects the club and swing (shot) he intends to play, 4) chooses a target, aims, and 5) swings away. The shot flies off and the cycle is complete. To start the next cycle, the golfer moves out to find the ball again.

This sounds simple, and fundamentally, it is simple. We add up the number of cycles (shots) it takes to get our ball into the cup on each hole, record this number on a scorecard, and move on to the next hole. One shot at a time … one hole at a time. At the end of the day, the total of our hole scores is our score for the round. This is golf.

1.1.2 Shots fly into patterns

The game would be incredibly simple (and boring) if every golfer hit every shot perfectly. We all know, however, shots don't always fly in the exact directions or distances we plan them to. Instead, we scatter shots around our intended targets. Think about it. How often have you hit a shot perfect enough to go into the cup?

Your shots usually land, bounce, roll and stop some distance away from your intended target; the lower your handicap, the smaller your misses (in general). If instead of playing one shot from each position on a hole, what if you hit 100? You probably wouldn't hole many, and you would see a pattern of balls around each target you chose. These would be your shot-patterns; an exact picture of where you hit shots in the past, and a statistical picture of where you are likely to hit shots with those clubs in the future.

Before we proceed, let me assure you of something:

1) Shot-patterns are real. They exist for all golfers. Your shots fly in shot-patterns from every club in your bag. Your shot-patterns can be improved and changed over time, but for now … they are what they are.

2) In measuring on-course play of both amateurs and pros for many years, I've found shot-patterns to be a good measure of their skill level (on practice ranges too, if measured properly), in each area of their game. The tighter your shot-pattern, the better (more skilled) you are in any given area.

Every shot goes somewhere. Imagine you could plot where every one of your last 100 fairway shots with a 7-iron ended up relative to their target, by a dot on paper. I know you can't really remember them, but imagine you could. You would see something like Figure 1.1.2.1 (x = start point for each shot, flagstick = target). Of course every golfer has their own unique skill level (some slice, some hook, some hit lots of fat shots, some don't) and shot-pattern for each club.

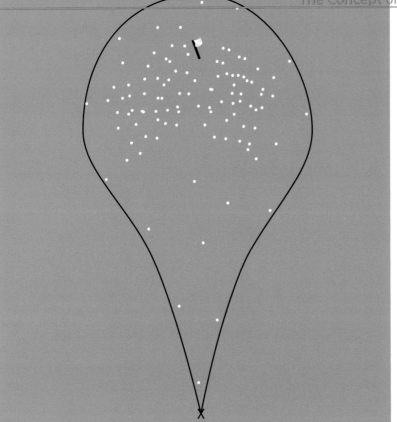

1.1.2.1

Shot Patterns

Shot-patterns are the golf equivalent of signatures. Every one is different for every player (and every club and type of shot). In general, individual golfers do not scatter their shots symmetrically around targets. Any particular golfer tends to miss left, short, or right, depending upon whether his swing weakness tends to make him pull/hook shots left, hit them fat and short, or slice them to the right.

The details of what shot patterns actually look like for real golfers can be found in one of my earlier books, "Dave Pelz's Short Game Bible", for those interested. For the purposes of Damage Control however, we use generic shot-pattern shapes in our illustrations (as shown in Figures 1.1.2.1 above and 1.1.2.2 next page) assuming a golfer who scatters his shots somewhat symmetrically. Note: in later illustrations, we will show only the outlines of shot-patterns, eliminating the balls for clarity.

To gain knowledge of what your own shot-patterns look like, how they are shaped and which way they are biased, you will have to perform some of the tests suggested in Chapter 7, and observe your own results.

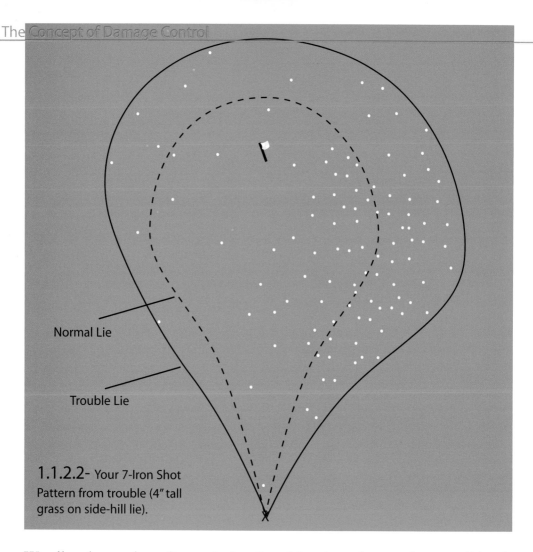

Normal Lie

Trouble Lie

1.1.2.2- Your 7-Iron Shot Pattern from trouble (4" tall grass on side-hill lie).

We all make good, mediocre, bad and awful swings, hitting shots in all kinds of directions and trajectories from all kinds of lies. Few golfers however are aware of how large their shot-patterns are from normal fairway lies. More importantly from a Damage Control perspective, most golfers have no idea of how their shot-patterns degrade when hitting from trouble lies (Figure 1.1.2.2).

The size of your shot-pattern measures the skill level with each club similar to the way scores measure overall skill for the game. Of course, you need many shots to establish shot-patterns and remembering them is complicated, so don't worry about doing this. Simply remember that the skill you have in playing shots, from good lies and trouble, determines your shot-patterns.

1.1.3 Trouble lies are important

Golf courses are designed ... with trouble in mind. There are good reasons why shots end up in trouble, and there is a lot of trouble out there. Golf course architects entice us into trying shots they know will end up in trouble. They design holes to challenge and test both the physical and mental abilities of golfers who play their masterpieces. They do this by offering a generally safe and beautiful pathway to play along, providing we hit nearly perfect shots. As we hit shots with less precision and more scatter, however, they present us with lies and conditions which graduate from marginally difficult to seriously difficult to extremely difficult and even to penalty strokes.

Golf courses penalize errant shots with lies in long grass, slopes, water, trees, rocks, bushes, sand, and innumerable other trouble situations. **In Damage Control we consider the lie of a ball to include ALL conditions of play which surround it.** Therefore, when we consider the lie of a shot, we include the tree limb which might be in the way of a backswing, the lip of the bunker in front of the ball, or the side-slope a golfer may have to stand on. In this context we have segregated lie conditions into four degrees of difficulty (safe, marginal, frying-pan and fire lies), and assigned a "difficulty-to-hit" number on a scale from zero to ten (ten being the most difficult). We also assign a characteristic color to each degree of difficulty. This "Lie-Difficulty" Scale (Figure 1.1.3.1 next page) is based on how difficult it is to hit a shot from a particular lie condition.

Although you can imagine the lie conditions and shots described in the Lie-Difficulty chart, their designations as safe (green), marginal (yellow), frying-pan (orange) and fire (red) areas may be unfamiliar to you. Make sure to examine the characteristics and descriptions in this scale as I will bring significance to these designations and colors throughout the rest of this chapter.

Lie

1.1.3.1

Degree of Difficulty	Color	Characteristics	Description
Safe (1,2)		-on the tee -on the fairway -on the green -on the green fringe	**Safe Lies** are from which the normal, no trouble game is played; as good as it gets.
Marginal (3-5)		-sitting up in light rough -good lie in green-side sand -on slight 2% slope -good lie in 4" rough	**Marginal Lies** include some degree of difficulty over normal safe lies, but should not cause significant problems in scoring.
Frying-Pan Trouble (6-8)		-nesty lie in grass -down lie in 4" rough -sloping terrain 4% up, down or side -6" rough	**Frying-Pan Trouble Lies** involve at least one degree of serious trouble, sometimes several, which leave the next shot possible but difficult to pull off without losing one or more strokes on your score, while being easy to hit badly into even worse trouble.
Fire Trouble (9,10)		-tree limbs and tall grass -sloping terrain 5% up, down or side -buried lie in sand with high lip -knee high weeds; strong grass -creek banks, deep woods, shallow water at edges of ponds	**Fire Trouble Lies** are really bad problems all the way around, may be difficult to get the ball back into play, in the extreme. taking an unplayable lie penalty maybe better than trying to hit out.

1.1.4 Golf as Seen through Dave Pelz's Eyes

Start by looking at an aerial view of a typical golf hole (Figure 1.1.4.1) in normal color. This should look familiar, being the colors you normally see when you look at a golf hole. Now look at the same hole through my eyes, the way I see holes (Figure 1.1.4.2). This view makes it immediately obvious where the safe areas are and where trouble is, with each area identified by its appropriate Lie-Difficulty color. I'm not trying to scare you with this view, but I like it because it allows me to see in a glance the situation a hole actually presents. This helps me make plans to play it the best way I can.

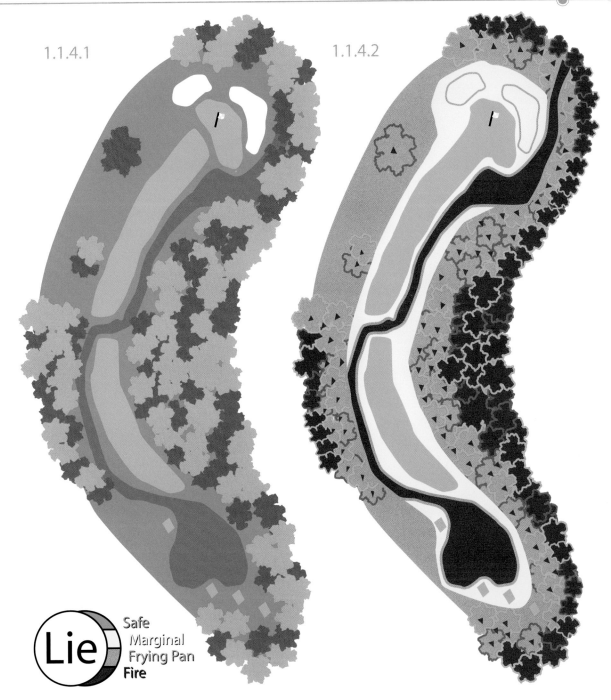

1.1.4.1

1.1.4.2

Lie
Safe
Marginal
Frying Pan
Fire

In terms of safe (green), we are talking about the relatively safe lies you generally get on the tees, fairways, fringes and greens. As you stray from safe areas into greenside and fairway sand bunkers, light rough and low-level slopes, these are marginal (yellow) areas. They present golfers with marginally more difficult lies to play from than safe lies.

More serious rough, trees, deep and/or sloping sand traps, valleys with up/down slopes and combinations of these conditions qualify as frying-pan (orange) areas. They represent significantly more difficult lies, stances and swing conditions from which it is easier to hit a bad shot out of the frying-pan … into the fire (from a bad lie, into an even worse lie). Fire (red) lies are defined as the really-bad to awful conditions of severely sloped gullies, tall weeds, deep grass, creek banks, ditches, ponds, mud, lakes, up-against fences, plus any other almost-impossible lie from which it is extremely difficult to escape.

Are you surprised that most of golf is not green and safe? Don't be; because this view … more trouble than safe … is generally true for most courses. Of course the exact trouble/safe area ratio is unique to every course, even to different holes on the same course.

Imagine how much yellow, orange and red you would see in a lie-difficulty color view, when looking down the super-narrow fairways of a U.S. Open Championship course. A truly difficult course presents far more trouble to the golfer than the local municipal course, which specializes in providing safe (and fast) playing conditions.

My point in showing you this (lie-difficulty) view of golf is to make you aware of how much trouble exists. Your association of color with trouble in your mind's eye (green = safe, yellow = marginal, orange = frying-pan, red = fire) will be useful later, in using the Damage Controller.

1.1.5 Skill level controls shot-patterns

Now that you know what golf courses really look like, and understand shots really fly into shot-patterns, let's see how skill level affects golfer's results. Look at a typical amateur 4-wood shot-pattern (imagine it might be yours) along side a pattern of the best 4-wood player I've ever seen, Phil Mickelson (Figure 1.1.5.1). Notice I've left out all the shots themselves and outlined the shapes of these two shot patterns. Phil's good 4-woods are longer and straighter than yours, and he hits a higher percentage of good ones than you. You on the other hand, hit more shots into marginal, frying-pan and fire lies than he does. He must be the better 4-wood player (Figure 1.1.5.2).

1.1.5.1 - The World's Best 4-wood Player

Your 4-wood shot pattern

Phil's 4-wood shot pattern

1.1.5.2

What happens when we move both you and Phil from safe lies into frying-pan trouble with your same 4-woods (Figure 1.1.5.3)? As you might expect from trouble, performance degrades for all golfers, because trouble (uneven ground, grass between clubface/ball, tree limb interference) changes the way swings must be made, away from the way they've been practiced. From frying-pan lies it's natural to expect fewer good swings, and more bad swings, from anybody.

Your 4-wood shot pattern
(frying pan lie)

Phil's 4-wood shot pattern
(frying pan lie)

1.1.5.3

Trouble lies cause troubled swings and troubling results. The majority of your practice has been spent hitting shots from perfect lies on level practice ground. It's no surprise this doesn't help your play from trouble. Look at how trouble affects shots:

1) Tall grass, clumps and weeds affect a golfer's ability to get the clubface cleanly on the ball at impact
2) Surrounding bushes, trees, banks or fences affect a golfer's ability to swing normally
3) Sloped and undulating terrain upset a golfers' stance and balance
4) Swing rhythm and timing are degraded by any (or combinations) of the above factors
5) Aiming (target selection) is difficult when you can't predict how shots will fly

Every golfer is human and no human is perfect. We all make good swings and bad ones, even from perfect lies. However, understand this: Pros handle trouble lies way better than amateurs (Figure 1.1.5.4). Notice how much smaller Mickelson's change in shot pattern is (green vs red) than yours.

1.1.5.4

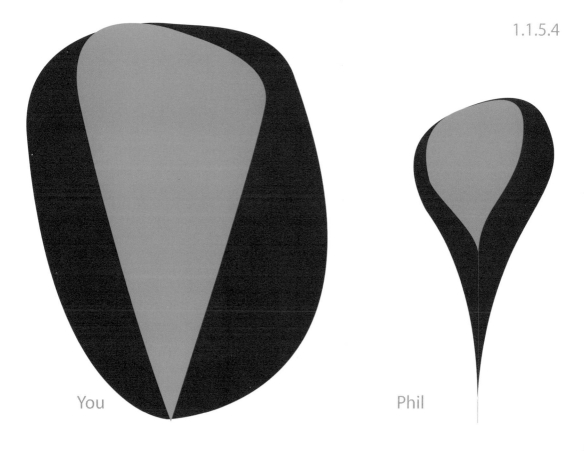

You   Phil

Recognition of this phenomenon … trouble affects amateurs disproportionately more than pros … is important for you to understand. Pros get out of trouble on their first try, amateurs don't. It's no coincidence amateurs record disaster scores frequently, pros record them rarely.

1.1.6 Target selection

Where golfers aim their shots is as important as how well they hit them. Where to aim shots depends on the size and shape of your expected shot pattern. Once you've located your ball, evaluated its lie, selected your club and know what kind of swing you can make, you're ready to think about how aggressively you want to choose your target. From perfect lies in the fairway this choice can be important. For shots from trouble, your target choice is critical. It affects, even determines, your chance of successful escape … or disaster.

You may be a golfer who normally plays conservatively from good lies, and already chooses safe targets when playing from trouble. Or you may be a riverboat gambler, who cannot resist trying almost impossible shots. In either case, your target selections will fall into one of four categories: Conservative, Aggressive, Risky or Dangerous (Figure 1.1.6.1).

In the Target Selection Chart the colors green, yellow, orange and red again represent shots that end up in safe, marginal, frying-pan or fire conditions of play, respectively. The relative density of colors in each spectral band represents the probability of your shot ending up in those conditions of play.

Conservative target choices are those which receive and retain shots in safe lies about 80% of the time. Of course the higher your skill level, the higher your percentage of shots will end up safe to any given target. So, an aggressive target for you may be a conservative choice for a multiple Major Championship winner like Phil Mickelson.

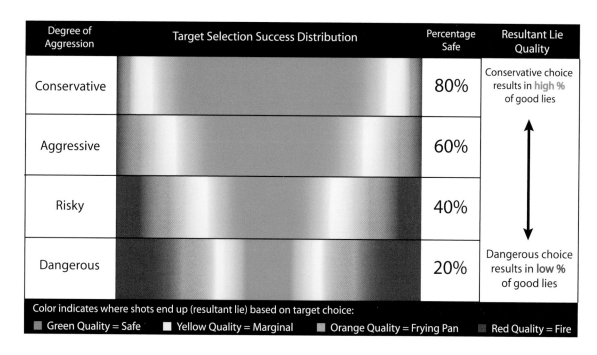

Degree of Aggression	Target Selection Success Distribution	Percentage Safe	Resultant Lie Quality
Conservative		80%	Conservative choice results in **high %** of good lies
Aggressive		60%	
Risky		40%	
Dangerous		20%	Dangerous choice results in **low %** of good lies

Color indicates where shots end up (resultant lie) based on target choice:
■ Green Quality = Safe   ■ Yellow Quality = Marginal   ■ Orange Quality = Frying Pan   ■ Red Quality = Fire

If the chance of your escape shot ending up in a safe lie is only 60%, you are choosing an aggressive target. When you choose a 40% chance-of-safe shot, you are making a risky choice. And when you try a shot you believe will turn out safe only 20% of the time, your target selection is classified as dangerous. (If you choose a less-than-10% probability of safe target, your strategy is reckless and we don't have a color for that.)

On a well designed course it is frequently the case where the closer you aim to the flagstick, the more dangerous the shot becomes. This is especially true for shots from trouble lies, which usually don't have much backspin, and fly into larger shot-patterns. If you understand what the target selection colors are telling you … "the more green a target choice has = the greater the chances of hitting the ball there safely" … you understand their meaning!

1.1.7 The overview connection

What is the relevance of all this? It means a golfer's lie, skill level, shot-pattern, and target selection all play a part (connect) in determining how he performs any particular shot, all over the golf course. When strung together shot after shot, these same factors combine to determine how he scores. And when the golfer finds trouble, these factors not only degrade, they degrade dramatically. They degrade so drastically they could even cause a problem in scoring.

A golf ball in trouble is like a snowball

Like a snowball getting larger as it rolls down a hill, there can be an "avalanche" effect from trouble lies:

1) Trouble lies on uneven terrain affect a golfer's set-up and posture
2) Troubled set-ups and posture (never before practiced) degrade a golfer's swing
3) As swings degrade in trouble, shot-patterns expand exponentially
4) Target selection is critical from trouble (if you don't know where your shot is going, you can't possibly know where to aim)

Most golfers think their normal swing skills from normal lies completely determine their scores and handicaps. They believe if they groove their swing on the practice tee, they can avoid trouble on the course, and avoid disaster scores. They are wrong.

They are not aware of:
       1) How much trouble exists on golf courses
       2) How often they are in trouble (every round)
       3) How poorly they perform from trouble lies
       4) How consistently their bad shots from trouble lead to disasters

---

1.1.7.1: Pelz Golf Institute: Research Conclusions

Tournament score cards from DuPont (2003) and PGA Tour Superstore (2004) World Amateur Handicap Championships, Myrtle Beach, South Carolina

Golfers:
1) Play most of each round (14 –17 holes) well below their handicap on a few holes disaster strikes and ruins their score for the day
2) Blame a few errant shots, bad bounces and/or bad breaks for getting into trouble
3) Often say they played well, but scored badly
4) Believe "getting into trouble" caused their disaster scores
5) Vow to practice normal swing more, so they can stay out of trouble
6) Don't recognize disaster holes as recurring part of their normal game

---

Golfers don't "get" what their scoring problem is, or that they even have a problem (Figure 1.1.7.1). They don't understand disaster scoring is a consistent problem in their games, and they aren't looking for an answer to this problem. They aren't aware that when their lie gets worse, their swings get much worse, and their shot patterns get exponentially worse. They don't know the set-up postures and swings required from trouble lies are different from those normally used and practiced, and they don't realize where their shots are going to go when they execute really bad swings from trouble lies.

A few times each round, golfers hit a shot into trouble and unwittingly use the exact recipe for disaster scoring. They swing from an unusual posture on poor terrain, attempt a swing they've never practiced before, aim at a target they have almost no chance of reaching … and hit shots out of the frying-pan … into the fire … and disaster!

1.2 Why Disasters Happen ... and Damage Control

OK, you've seen an overview of the game, and we've established a few concepts which help understand how it is played. You understand how the lie of the ball (safe, marginal, frying-pan, fire) interplays with a golfer's skill level, shot-pattern and target selection (conservative, aggressive, risky, dangerous) to determine his scoring results. And you're aware of how drastically trouble affects amateurs, compared to pros.

It's time to look at why this all happens, and learn what can be done about it. The truth is PGA Tour professionals don't have too much of a problem with trouble lies, and you shouldn't either. I say this because I already know about Damage Control and what it can do for you. You don't understand this yet, but hang-on ... you will!

1.2.1 Trouble is good

Trouble is good. The game wouldn't be as much fun or exciting without it. Courses are designed to get you into trouble, and to test how you escape from it. It's part of the challenge. Good course design graduates from providing safe to marginal, frying-pan, and fire lies for your shots, as your swings go from good to bad to awful. Architects design holes to also mix in both good and bad luck. This makes for the wonderful and sometimes euphoric (when good luck comes) game we all play and love.

Golfers make bad swings from time to time. Even from perfect lies the best players in the world occasionally hit shots into serious trouble (Figures 1.2.1.1 to 1.2.1.3). You must assume then, that you, too, will hit shots into trouble.

Your mediocre, bad and awful swings are as much a part of your game as are your good swings (just not as frequent, thank heaven). And, they will get you into trouble on occasion. This means trouble is waiting for you, in your next round, and for the rest of your golf career. Embrace it, it's part of your game, and it's good.

How should you deal with trouble? The best way is not to spend all your time trying to avoid it, because that can't be done. The better way is to learn to get out of it (learn Damage Control) without letting it ruin your score.

1.2.1.1

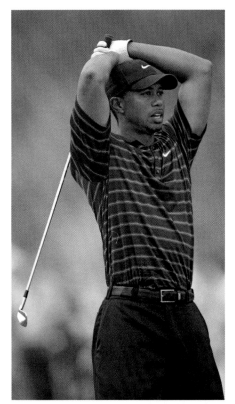

1.2.1.1 - 1.2.1.3 (clockwise from top)-

1.2.1.1 - 18th tee (Whistling Straits)

1.2.1.2 - Retief in trouble (ball in the bushes next to a stone wall) at the 11th hole of Royal Troon Golf Club (2004 Open Championship)

1.2.1.3 - Tiger's reaction after an errant shot during the final round of the 2005 Tour Championship

1.2.1.3   1.2.1.2

1.2.2 Out of the frying pan … into the fire

Let's examine what happens from a trouble lie. Assume you drive your ball into a frying-pan trouble lie. If your next swing is well-executed to a safe target, it should propel your ball out from the trouble, back into the game in a better position than where a good drive would have been in the first place. In this case you probably post an acceptable score on the hole, and no real harm comes to your round. This is what happens after most errant shots in a normal round of golf.

If however, your shot following your drive into trouble does not escape from that trouble, and in fact flies into worse trouble, you have essentially jumped out of the frying pan … into the fire. It's easy to make a bad swing from a trouble lie. Once you play from the frying-pan into the fire, it's even easier to play a worse shot into an impossible situation. This sequence takes you from bad to worse, spiraling down and down, into a true disaster-hole. The sequence sometimes even leads to a "ball in pocket" … the ultimate disaster, a completely ruined, aborted round.

Every trouble lie presents a potential for disaster. The scenario described above defines the pathway to disaster: From the frying pan … to the fire … to disaster. Unfortunately, this sometimes happens several times in the same round. Trouble lies are part of the game by design, they have to be. But bungled escape attempts, fire lies, and disaster scores don't have to be!

Another pathway to disaster is brought into play when golfers try "hero" recovery shots from trouble. They've seen Tiger and Phil hit these shots, so they try them too. The hero shot requires a trajectory so precise that even a relatively-good swing can seldom carry it off (Figure 1.2.2.1). Hero shots rarely turn out well, and more often than not, initiate an excellent opportunity for disaster.

1.2.3 Have you seen your shot-patterns from trouble?

Remember, every shot goes somewhere. Everybody is human. We all have shot-patterns with bad shots in them, even from perfect lies in the fairway (even from the tee). It's also true none of us are immune to bad bounces, which sometimes get us into trouble … even after we've executed good swings and launched good shots.

There is worse news however. Everyone's shot-patterns, regardless of skill level or handicap, get worse when playing from difficult trouble conditions. If you think about it, this makes sense. Obviously the scatter of our shot-patterns will be worse for shots hit from difficult stances and bad lies we never practice, compared to those hit from perfectly level fairway lies we practice all the time (and take lessons on).

Look at the positions players get themselves into when trying to extricate their balls from trouble (Figures 1.2.3.1 through 1.2.3.3). Can you imagine where some of these shots go? (Believe me, they don't all turn out perfect!)

1.2.3.1 - Brad Faxon at the Swilken Burn, St Andrews (2005 Open Championship)

1.2.3.2 – Phil Mickelson looking for his ball and blasting out of tall grass at the 2004 U.S. Open Championship at Shinnecock Hills Golf Club

1.2.3.3 – Sergio Garcia hitting out of trouble during the 2000 Eurobet Seve Ballesteros Trophy between Continental Europe and Great Britain/Ireland at Sunningdale Golf club in Sunningdale, England

How often do you practice from these kinds of conditions, and do you know how to change your swing to produce good shots from them? Your honest answers are probably "never", and "I have no idea". This proves my point: You don't know what your shot-patterns from such circumstances look like!

Imagine if you were asked to create your shot-pattern from any trouble lie on the right side of the 18th green at the famed Pinehurst #2 (Figure 1.2.3.4). If 100 balls were thrown into that area with some of them in the bunker, close to the large lip, while others were near the bunker edges and others ended up near me - on a slight downhill lie to a tight pin, how close to the pin do you think you would hit them? Think especially where the shots from the downhill lies would fly, when you have a green like an upside-down saucer with balls running away as they near the edges. Have you ever run a test like this, hitting practice shots, just to see where the balls go?

Most golfers haven't, and they have absolutely no clue where their shots are going when they hit them with swings they've never tried before, from stances they've never swung from before. How can anyone possibly plan and play reasonable escape shots from trouble, when they have no idea where the ball is going when they hit it?

1.2.3.4

1.2.4 Failed escapes equal disaster

Our research results are very clear. First we discovered most golfers waste 2 to 5 shots each round on disaster holes, while playing the rest of their holes relatively well. Next, we discovered the initial bad shots which get into trouble are usually not the shots that cause disaster scores. Instead, it's the shot that follows the errant shot that causes disaster. When this following shot fails to escape from the trouble it's in, and instead moves the ball out of the frying pan … into the fire, it becomes the true culprit and source of disaster scoring.

I'll say this again (because it's important): Disaster scores are not caused by errant shots which get into trouble. Research shows golfers get away with most of those. Rather, it is the next shot, **the failed escape shot** which gets into worse trouble than it started from, that causes disaster holes.

Have you ever asked yourself: "How often do my escape shots go out of the frying pan … into the fire? And do I know why those shots didn't turn out, causing disaster scores"?

If you are like most golfers, your answers are:
>   1) Maybe once in almost every round, and
>   2) No, I simply hit the ball so poorly it went sideways … I don't know why I put such an awful swing on it!

<u>**Disaster scores are not caused by errant shots which get into trouble. They are caused by escape shots which fail to get out of trouble.**</u>

1.2.5 Normal swings don't work from trouble

There are good reasons why golfers make poor swings from trouble lies. Detailed testing has shown that amateur golfers lack knowledge of one or all of the following:

1) How their posture on un-even terrain affects their swing
2) How to alter their swing shape, to miss obstructions
3) How the ball will behave after it comes out of trouble

1.2.5.1

Let me show you examples of this:

1) If a high-lofted, open-faced cut-wedge shot is needed to pitch a shot over sand from a severe downhill lie … a normal swing with a wedge will not do the job (Figure 1.2.5.1 above). From a normal posture with your spine vertical, a normal swing will almost surely hit the ground behind the ball (right).

2) When a golfer needs a flat swing to hit a ball from under a tree … using a normal swing that tips the tree and deflects the club off-line is no good (Figure 1.2.5.2).

3) When backspin is impossible to impart to a shot from tall grass, golfers should not try dangerous shots to a fast green with the flag on a down slope (Figure 1.2.5.3). Instead they should play away from the pin rolling the ball down the hill in a different (and safer) direction.

Using the wrong swing or playing the wrong shot, the odds of escaping safely from trouble are not in your favor! Golfers routinely attempt to use normal-lie swings from trouble, and expect normal shot behavior in terms of backspin and stopping ability. This often results in bad shots getting into even worse trouble, and the disaster scores that follow.

Every time golfers get into trouble, it seems different – because it usually is different! They've never received instruction on setting-up or making swings in trouble, never practiced from these conditions, and never noticed how shots react from such lies. Golfers simply don't know how to make the swings and shots that will effectively escape from trouble. These are the facts.

1.2.6 Escape skills exist

Pros do it … you can too. The knowledge and skill to execute successful escape swings exists, and is part of what we have developed and teach in Damage Control.

We have measured, tested, and without doubt proven this fact: faced with a ball 12 inches above or below their stance, most golfers cannot hit a shot anywhere near where they are aiming. The same is true for up and downhill lies, tall grass lies, balls embedded in sand, under tree limbs, next to bushes, on hard-pan dirt, and a myriad of other troubled conditions we all (sooner or later) get ourselves into.

The truth of the matter is:

1) Most golfers don't realize normal swings don't work from trouble
2) Many aren't aware of how to change their swings to hit escape shots from trouble
3) Special swings for escape from trouble lies are not taught by most golf professionals
4) Golfers don't realize trouble shots don't usually spin or stop like normal shots

Even after you understand all of this, you still may say to yourself; "I can't hit the ball well enough from good lies to stay out of trouble. Why not practice my normal swing and make it better, rather than work on learning something new like Damage Control?" This is a mistake however. No golfer has ever, in the entire history of golf, learned to avoid trouble on the golf course, and you are not likely to be the first!

Even if you devote the rest of your life to improving your normal game, you'll still find trouble, and Damage Control can help you get out of it without ruining your score.

Normal practice doesn't prepare us. No matter how much you practice on the range from "flat-terrain-perfect" lies (Figure 1.2.6.1a) it probably won't help you when you get into trouble situations (Figure 1.2.6.1b). It's also of no help that most practice facilities do not offer golfers the chance to practice from trouble-lie conditions. The net is, most golfers don't practice the set-ups, swings, or shots needed to escape from trouble in real scoring situations.

1.2.6.1A   1.2.6.1B

1.2.7 The development of Damage Control

Damage Control is a new and different-from-normal skill of golf. It is also a real, meaningful, and important skill to learn. Previously golfers only thought about trouble in terms of working on their normal game, to play better and stay out of it.

Staying out of trouble is impossible however. No one will ever do it! The rulers of the game (the U.S.G.A.) keep setting up courses to play longer, tighter, harder, and faster, to make sure everyone, even the pros, get into trouble. No matter how much better golfers learn to hit their shots, this is as it should be; trouble lies will always and forever be part of the game!

By studying golfers' play from trouble, we've learned what must be done to get out successfully. We've measured why they are so bad at hitting trouble shots, and how they don't understand where their shots are going after they hit them. As a result, we've developed Damage Control as:

a) Five learnable Damage Control skills (Figure 1.2.7.1)
b) Drills to practice and develop Damage Control skills (Chapter 7), and
c) A fundamental philosophy: By escaping from trouble on your first try, to a place better than your previous shot would have been had it been good, you should lose less than one stroke … and almost never encounter disasters.

1.2.7.1 - The Five Skills of Damage Control

- Set-up-ology (Chapter 2: How to Set-up to trouble shots)
- Swing Shaping (Chapter 3: How to shape your swings in trouble)
- Hand-Fire Feel (Chapter 4: Using your hands in escape shots)
- Red-Flag Touch (Chapter 5: Learning how escape shots behave once they land)
- Damage Control Mentality (Chapter 6: Using the Damage Controller)

1.2.7.2

In Damage Control, like in horse-shoes, close counts. One of the nice things about Damage Control is your swings don't have to be perfect. They just have to be good enough (reasonably solid) to escape from trouble and get the ball back into the game. If you get back into a safe lie, in a better position (blue area) than the previous errant shot (red "X") would have been had it been perfect (black "X") (Figure 1.2.7.2), you've done it. And Damage Control will lower your scores without changing your normal game skills, swings, practice techniques or habits.

1.3 Almost Avoid Disasters … Forever!

Almost is a big word. No one can avoid disasters completely forever. Luck plays too great a part in golf, and we're all human. We all make bad swings. For all golfers, sometime, somewhere, you will make a disaster score on a disaster hole. But this doesn't mean disasters have to be a normal part of your game!

1.3.1 Have you seen the Damage Controller?

We developed this little beauty (Figure 1.3.1.1) at the Pelz Golf Institute. It's small, simple to use, and very expensive. It's taken a long time to get into this form, and I only have one. It's so valuable to me you can't buy it, but when I show you how to use it (in Chapter 6) you'll learn something valuable. For now, let me show you what it does.

Look carefully at the series of photos in Figure 1.3.1.2 on the next few pages and follow three steps of how the Damage Controller works:

1.3.1.1

Step #1: (a) I turn on the Damage Controller (push "Lie" button) to show it an overview of the trouble I'm in, then ...

(b) I show it a close-up view of the lie and any swing limitations involved around the ball.

(c) = Immediately, the screen shows me which shot (club and swing) I can best play in this situation and how difficult that shot will be.

- CLUB **SW**

- SHOT **1/2 upright**

- DIFFICULTY **6**

Step #2: (d) = After seeing my shot, I push the "Skill" button to allow the Damage Controller to calculate and show me an outline of the shot pattern I can expect from these conditions.

- CLUB **SW**
- SHOT **1/2 upright**
- DIFFICULTY **6**

Step #3: I aim the Damage Controller at a landing area I'm considering for the shot, and push the "Target" button. This gives me a view of the target in a terribly exciting way. It shows my shot-pattern distributed around the target with the percentage scale and number of shots which will end up in safe lies (along the right; 20 % in this case). It also overlays a color scale (e) to show me how safe … or dangerous … that target is to hit to!

- CLUB SW

- SHOT 1/2 upright

- DIFFICULTY 6

Isn't that outrageous? Can you imagine? No matter the difficulty of my lie, the Damage Controller knows my ability to execute swings, and how my shots will fly (my shot-patterns). It also uses highly sophisticated computer technology to calculate the odds of my shot making it to a safe lie in the target area (number at top right). Simultaneously, it shows me the relative probability of shots landing in safe (green), marginal (yellow), frying-pan (orange) and fire (red) lies, with its color spectrum.

Preposterous you say? Absolutely not I say! The Damage Controller has an incredible optics system and computer inside it. It can remember all my shots from previous trouble (it has a very large memory chip). It's seen me hit shots from all kinds of trouble, and exactly what happened in each and every case (how I swung, where the shots went). This information is stored in memory, and used in its predictions. This all may sound incredible to you … but believe it. By the end of this book you'll see I'm telling you the truth, and you'll know my Damage Controller is real, and works like I'm telling you.

1.3.2 Wouldn't it be nice to know?

Wouldn't you like to have this knowledge when you're in trouble? Just imagine if you could buy a Damage Controller of your own, programmed completely for you and your game, and carry it with you on the course. Every time you were in some kind of trouble, you could pull out the Damage Controller and see how to best play your escape shot. You could look left of the creek, or under the tree limb, or wherever, moving the Damage Controller target view until it read an acceptable probability of success for hitting there. Then you'd know exactly where to aim your escape shot.

Wouldn't it be nice when you're in trouble to know what shot to try and exactly where you should aim, to have the highest probability of success in getting out? Please understand, even this incredibly valuable Damage Controller is not perfect. It can never tell you 100% for sure you will escape to your target spot in the fairway, just short of the green. It can only give you the odds of your getting there.

Even in a case where most of your swings would normally escape from trouble, your body might just decide to put an awful swing on the ball, and hit it straight to the right into fire trouble. The Damage Controller can tell you the odds of good shots vs. bad happening. It can't tell you which exact shot will happen. Also realize, to take advantage of a Damage Controller, you need the skills of making good Damage Control set-ups and swings.

1.3.3 Play with probable, not possible

For years I have been trying to convince Tour professionals to only attempt shots they believe they can pull off successfully 90% of the time. Why do I choose 90%? Because I've seen too many golfers try risky (40%) and dangerous (20% probability of escaping safely) shots, with disastrous results. Remember, the best players in the world make bad swings on occasion, and even they are not immune to the wrath of the golf gods when they combine trouble lies with poor swings and high risk targets.

At this point let me interject another piece of information garnered from research. In studying the play of both amateurs and professional golfers (almost without regard to skill level or handicap) I've found: if golfers think they can hit a shot, they will try it. And when I say can, I mean if they think they can possibly, or are physically capable of hitting the shot.

Too many golfers attempt shots they possibly-can hit, rather than those they probably-will hit. Golfers play the game expecting to hit the most perfect shot they are physically capable of hitting; rather than one of the shots out of their normal shot-pattern. They expect to hit their best shot when they need it, even when there is a penalty awaiting them if they don't.

What are they thinking? Do they think bad shots only come when they aren't trying to hit good shots? How many golfers do you know who try to hit bad shots? Of course we all try to hit good shots all the time ... but the bad ones still come. Nobody is perfect, and you must recognize your probability is to hit shots commensurate with your current shot-pattern. Your pattern can be improved over time, but "it is ... what it is" for now. In any situation, trouble or otherwise, you should play the game expecting and allowing for shots from your current shot-patterns.

1.3.4.1

1.3.4 Less aggressive is sometimes more aggressive

An example you may identify with is a 23 handicap alumnus of my Scoring Game School (who shall remain un-named). I had measured his driver shot-pattern and was invited to play a round with him. He swings hard, hits lots of long hooks and slices, and about twice in ten drives unleashes a really nice, long, straight one. We were on a very difficult 430-yard par-4 hole (which would take a perfect drive and perfect 5-iron for him), with out of bounds down the left and a lake along the right in the driving area (Figure 1.3.4.1). He hit a reasonably good, solid, 250-yard drive, which landed at least 20-yards into the water on the right.

To my amazement, he exclaimed "Damn it, I can't believe I hit that shot. I just can't get water out of my mind; it must be a mental thing. Water is like a magnet to me". As I looked at him and smiled, I visualized his driver shot-pattern on the practice range (with no water in sight). He had absolutely no recognition that at least 50% of the best drives from his drive-pattern would land in that water. To my way of thinking, he had just saved one stroke by at least not hitting it out of bounds to the left!

His expectation (hope) was to hit one of the few good straight drives he knows he possibly can hit, at just the right time. Would he ever consider hitting a 5-wood off the tee, safely short of the water, then another 5-wood to the green on this hole? Not a chance! When he stands on any tee, it's bombs away, no matter what lies ahead.

Less can be More

From trouble lies, sometimes less aggressive in target selection … is more aggressive in score hunting!

Even a tee can be trouble. You could think of this tee shot (Figure 1.3.4.1) with tight OB left and water right as being a frying-pan trouble shot, even though its lie was actually perfect. It presents a seriously difficult shot to a golfer who has a wild shot-pattern with the driver. Like a frying-pan lie, it offers plenty of opportunity to hit the ball into the fire, and make a disaster score. Even with three of his better swings, this fellow might create two water balls and one out-of-bounds. Just imagine where he aims and what swings he tries when hitting out of trouble! The lesson here: From frying-pan lies, less aggressive target selection is sometimes more aggressive score hunting.

1.3.5 Escape … then recover

A major tenant of Damage Control is you must escape from trouble before you recover from it. Think about this: when you escape from trouble with one swing, to a better position than you would have been in from a good shot in the first place, you are then free to make a good next (recovery) swing and save the stroke you were in danger of losing.

1.3.5.1A

To see this, look at the trouble situation in the Figure 1.3.5.1A-C series.

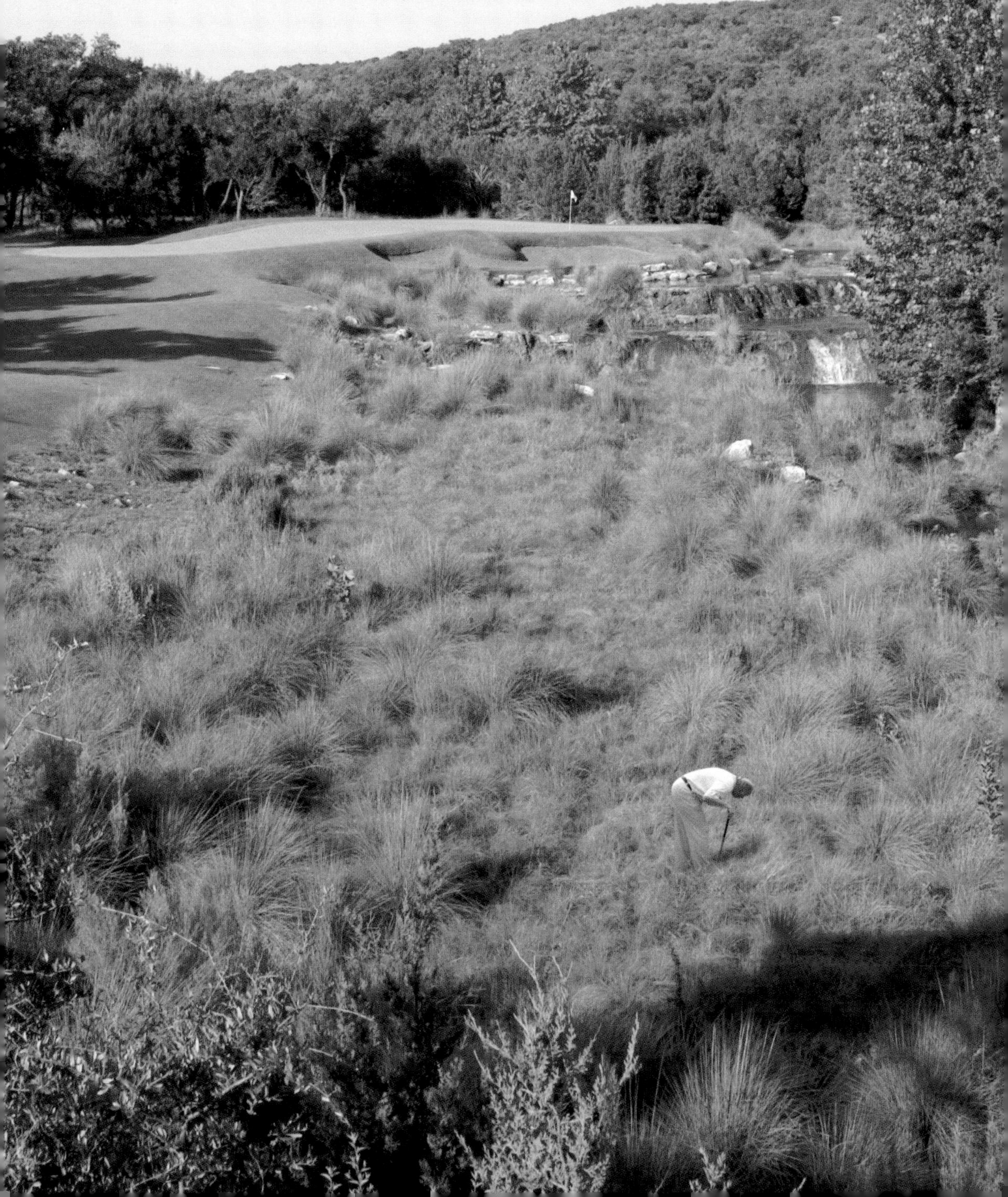

Too many golfers would try a miraculous recovery shot here, aim at the flagstick, hit the ball short or into the water and score at least 6 (Figure 1.3.51B).

1.3.5.1B

Instead, wouldn't it be smarter to acknowledge the trouble you are in, escape from it, then try to minimize the damage by getting up-and-down from the fairway short of the green to score a 4 or at worst 5 (Figure 1.3.5.1C)?

1.3.5.1C

Less than one-stroke

When you escape from trouble on the first try, getting back into the game in a better position than you would have been in from a good shot in the first place, you are free to recover and save the stroke you are in danger of losing.

Most golfers aren't aware of their shot-patterns from good lies on level ground, except in a very general way. Even fewer realize how bad (large) their shot-patterns become from trouble lies, so they are not aware of how easily they may move from the frying-pan into the fire.

1.3.6 Less than one stroke is key

To control damage you must accept this fact; every time you get into trouble, you will add a fraction of a shot to your score, on average. The lower you make that fraction, the better player you will become. In this regard, the farther forward you can advance your safe escape toward the green, the lower that fraction of a stroke lost should be (on occasion it can be zero, when you save the stroke with a one-putt).

There is seldom a reason you should lose more than one full stroke because you hit a shot into trouble. Just by escaping back into the game into a position ahead of where you should have been in the first place, you should be able to lose, on average, less than one shot.

The process of playing with Damage Control is not much different from the process you normally use on most shots (the fundamental cycle of golf). To see this, imagine you just hit an errant tee shot onto a side hill lie under a tree:

1) Show the Damage Controller your lie (assuming I'd let you borrow it, and had programmed it for you); let it evaluate the trouble and determine your best shot (club and swing)

2) Look into the Damage Controller to see the shot-pattern of your escape shot

3) Select the target for escape which gives you the combination of:
- A 90% certainty of successful escape to a safe lie
- A position closer to the green than your previous shot should have been in

4) Take a Damage Control set-up and stance, appropriate for your side hill lie

5) Make a Damage Control (flat or upright) swing which misses the tree limb

6) After your ball lands back in the game (out of trouble), focus on recovering to save the stroke you might lose due to the trouble you were in

1.4 Subtleties of Damage Control

Great players play with Damage Control. When you see them face difficult, challenging shots on television, they usually do quite well getting themselves free without losing strokes to par. They succeed because they've learned the skills of Damage Control through their own on-course experiences.

They've practiced the shots that cost them strokes, to be ready to better execute them in future tournaments. Based on vast experience (they all hit lots of bad shots into lots of trouble), Tour professionals have learned the set-up and posture, swing shape, hand action, touch, and target selection required to extricate balls from trouble on their first try on a regular basis. It is critical to their success to have these skills and to know what shot-patterns to expect from trouble lies.

1.4.1 Who needs Damage Control

Sam said it best: There is a famous story about a discussion between the great Sam Snead (Figure 1.4.1.1) and baseball's best-ever hitter Ted Williams. Each was making a case for the difficulty of his sport, when Snead said, "But Ted, in golf we have to play our foul balls." Sam got it right. In golf you have to play your foul balls, and it helps when you do so with Damage Control!

1.4.1.1 - Sam Snead

1.4.1.2

Damage Control is important because we all need to deal with trouble for as long as we play the game. Because you'll periodically make bad swings, and get occasional bad bounces, you never know when Damage Control will be needed to minimize the damage to your score. Disaster holes are not fun for anybody.

The best practice Damage Control. Vijay Singh, who may practice his normal swings more than anyone else, also practices his Damage Control skills (like Figure 1.4.1.2: a tough green-side lie with water behind the flag stick).

Vijay is a good example of how PGA Tour players play with Damage Control. He is an aggressive player and hits driver off most tees. Although he is very straight considering his distance, he drives his ball into trouble on almost every round he plays (I've walked many rounds with him, and believe me this is true). Once in trouble however, he plays with incredible escape skills, and seldom hits shots from the frying pan into the fire. His escape shots usually get him into a position from which his wonderful short game skills can eliminate the potential lost stroke.

This is in contrast to average golfers who try difficult recovery shots from trouble, and all too often hit into even worse trouble. A gigantic difference between the games of professional golfers and weekend players, are the skills of Damage Control. Once you learn these skills (and you can learn them relatively easily), you can begin to bridge this gap.

1.4.2 Damage Control makes the game easier

Scoring seems difficult to golfers (and maybe to you) because most golfers try to play the game without having the proper tools. Trying to get out of trouble with normal swings is like trying to do a home repair without the right tool. Like when you try unscrewing a screw without a screwdriver? Or pound a nail without a hammer? I hope you see what I mean.

Once you have the skills of Damage Control, there's no reason why you cannot:
- Play from uphill-plugged bunker lies
- Splash the ball out of water hazards
- Hit under tree limbs, off hardpan, pine needles, or cart paths
- Blast shots from U.S. Open-style rough

All Damage Control requires is swinging "good-enough" to escape on your first try. Notice I didn't say you have to hole your shots from trouble. You simply must get them back into play on the first try!

There are thrills in golf you shouldn't miss. I realize it's fun to try, and occasionally pull off, miracle shots. When your score is not important and you have plenty of time and golf balls, you should "go for them". Try to execute the miraculous recovery shot. It can truly be a thrill and worth the expense.

I warn you, however, against trying these shots when your score really counts. It's easy to get addicted to the thrill of the "almost-impossible"; so be careful. It can work itself insidiously into your attitude, and if it ever gets in there, it will cost you dearly, both in your scores and handicap.

Saving Strokes

You'll probably save more strokes from learning Damage Control in three weeks, than from practicing your long iron swing for three years.

I often hear the following question from students: "Why should I practice Damage Control when my normal game is so bad? Wouldn't I be better off to learn to hit the ball better, so I can avoid trouble in the first place?"

The answer is NO! The inadequacies in your normal game are the reason you need Damage Control! The worse your normal game, the more you need and will benefit from Damage Control. Damage Control will stay with you always. Your normal game is never going to be good enough to avoid trouble completely. Even the best players in the game still find trouble in almost every round they play. Trouble is designed into the game, and you need to learn to make the best of it.

Damage Control will improve your scores, no matter how good the rest of your game gets. It will save you strokes in your next round, and for the rest of your career.

1.4.3 When is Damage Control needed?

In every round you play, every time your ball finds trouble, you need Damage Control. You need it to bring your good scores all the way to the house (sign your 18-hole card without disaster holes), lower your handicap, score the best you can on any given day, and smile as you walk off the 18th green.

If you are a professional, Damage Control can help you win more tournaments, miss fewer cuts, lower your scoring average, and win major championships. If scoring is important to you, you need Damage Control, but don't try to extend it over the entire golf course. Level lies in light rough are in-the-game. Damage Control is necessary only when you worry about hitting the next shot into worse trouble than you're already in (sloping terrain, deep grass, trees, water, bad sand lies, etc.).

Not on the practice range. Normal practice time on the normal flat range is for your normal swings. Damage Control development is not to be substituted for this. You can't practice the swings of Damage Control when you're on the perfectly level fairway cut of the practice range anyway. When you practice normal swing techniques, don't even think about Damage Control.

If you want to score better the next round you play, work on your Damage Control skills immediately. I know you're going to get into trouble in your upcoming round and I want you to get out of it without ruining your score. Don't cancel any lessons you have scheduled with your pro; just do your Damage Control work first. Then you'll have the best of both worlds, playing better for most of your round, plus getting out of trouble when you stumble into it!

1.4.4 Develop Damage Control in your own backyard

Damage Control is not about eliminating errant shots. You are a golfer, or you wouldn't be reading this book. You probably know about the golf swing, golf rules, golf courses, and maybe even about sports psychology. But when I ask my students the question "are you scoring as well as you can, for the conditions of your life-style and game?" most golfers answer absolutely not. Then they list their procrastinations, reasons and excuses for not practicing more, usually concluding – "really, I guess it's because I just don't practice enough".

If you believe this and think the only way to play better is to practice more and hit fewer errant shots, you are wrong. You can improve substantially and quickly by studying this book, then spending a few sessions in your own backyard. By practicing with feedback in your yard (details in Chapter 7), you can learn the feel of the Damage Control swings you need to develop.

Then you should play a couple of Damage Control practice rounds at your local course (again, details in Chapter 7). It will surprise you how much fun it is even though you won't post a score after it's over. I was amazed the first time I did it, not only by how much fun I had trying to hit all the crazy trouble shots I'd never practiced before, but also how immediately I benefited from it on my following rounds of play.

Before you worry about practicing Damage Control, however, you need to learn intellectually what you need to learn physically, about Damage Control. This means learning about the 5 skills of Damage Control presented in the next 5 Chapters.

Set-up-ology is the study of how to set-up for trouble shots. It's the first skill of Damage Control because golfers must set-up before taking their backswings, downswings or follow-throughs, and a bad set-up affects everything that follows. Whether it's an unusual stance on difficult terrain, something inhibiting the golfer's swing, or just "stuff" around the ball, trouble lies require different set-ups from normal. Dealing with how to set-up is often the first difficulty a golfer encounters in trouble.

Research shows awkward stances and poor set-ups create bad swings and shots which fly out of the frying pan ... into the fire for a high percentage of golfers. But data also indicate when golfers understand and internalize set-up-ology they improve their ability to escape from trouble dramatically.

Setting-up in bad posture for a trouble shot is like tying both hands behind your back before trying to swing. Even from perfect lies on level tees, bad set-ups make swinging properly difficult. But from a lie in difficult terrain with tree limbs in the way, taking a bad set-up is the golfing equivalent of shooting one's self in the foot.

2.1 Fundamentals of your "Normal" Swing

It has often been said: golf is a game of rolling balls, inclined planes, impacts and energy transfer ... a game of physics. While this is true, there is more to it than that. The position and alignment of the bones and joints in a golfer's body determine the swing force and power his muscles and motion can deliver to a ball at impact. So in this sense, it's also a game of body positions, muscles and inter-related body motions.

Every golfer tries to make perfect swings and hit perfect shots. When those swings and shots turn out to be "not-so-perfect", we take lessons and practice to improve them. These lessons often deal with our set-up positions, the shape of our swings, where we take divots, and how "upright" or "flat" we swing our clubs. The problem is; most of this practice time occurs on the flat and level practice ground of a practice range, and does nothing to improve Damage Control. Still, it helps to understand our normal swing before we try to improve our Damage Control swings from trouble.

2.1.1 It's difficult to make a good swing from a bad set-up

To make a good golf swing, one must be physically able to make good shoulder and hip turn motions, without hitting some outside interference. For example, your body can't make a good swing while lying on your back, because the ground won't allow you to rotate your shoulders or hips enough to create good motion (Figure 2.1.1.1a). The restriction provided by the ground is even more obvious when you see it rotated into an upright position (b). Once the ground is removed however, I can turn freely and make my normal driver swing (c).

2.1.1.1

A

B

C

It's also difficult to make effective swings without good balance, because losing balance means moving your body in strange ways and getting into really strange positions. Obviously, bad balance can destroy any golf shot (Figure 2.1.1.2).

2.1.1.2

2.1.2 The golf swing is not a circle

When viewed face-on, the cocking of your wrists relative to your forearms increases gradually as you swing back away from the ball. The wrists don't become fully cocked until near the top of the backswing or the start of the downswing, but stay fully cocked in the downswing until shortly before impact. This difference in wrist cock timing produces a larger radius for the arc of the club head on the backswing, as compared to the downswing (demonstrated by perhaps the greatest wedge player of all time, Tom Kite, Figure 2.1.2.1). This can have a dramatic effect on whether or not a golfer can make a backswing from some frying-pan or fire trouble situations, when some kind of obstacle is crowding in behind the golfer's ball.

2.1.2.1.

2.1.3 Every swing has a "bottom"

Every golfer's swing has a lowest point or "bottom" relative to the ground, where their normal divot occurs. Different players who have different swing timing and weight shift actions will have slightly different bottom (divot) positions, even on shots from level ground.

For a lie on level ground the divot of most golfers starts at about the middle of their stance, which means the center of their swing-arc bottoms-out about two to four inches forward of their stance center (Figure 2.1.3.1). The precise location of where a player's club will first strike the ground is sometimes dramatically affected by the terrain, stance and set-up of the player, and can have a significant effect on where their ball should be positioned (forward or back) in their stance.

2.1.3.1.

To insure clean contact with the little ball (golf ball) before contact with the big ball (earth), the little ball should always be positioned either exactly on or slightly behind where the golfer's divot will commence (not where the middle of the divot bottoms out, not in the middle of their stance, not anywhere in particular for all shots).

2.1.4 What's a swing plane?

If you track a golfer's clubhead throughout his swing, and the clubhead always travels in a single plane, that plane is called the golfer's swing plane. The angle measured between the plane and the ground is the player's swing plane angle. If you put a camera lens (or your eyes) behind a golfer in the plane of an in-plane swing, you'll see something like Kite's swing (Figure 2.1.4.1).

Golfers who swing their clubhead in the same plane on both their back and through-swings (and that plane also contains their sternum, shoulders and the ball at address), are said to be swinging in the so-called "perfect" swing plane. Although most golfers address shots with their hands somewhat below their swing plane, the faster they swing and the more clubhead speed they generate, the closer their hands come to moving up into their swing plane through impact.

2.1.4.1.

You can't "see" if a golfer is swinging "in plane" when standing behind them, unless your eyes are in the swing plane (which they will not be, if you are standing on the ball-to-target line). This means you can't tell if a golfer is swinging in the perfect swing plane from a photograph, unless you know the camera lens was positioned in that plane at the moment the photo was taken.

Many golfers have two distinct swing planes, one for their backswing, changing to a different plane for their down/through swing. Either one (or neither) of these planes may be the "perfect" plane. Other golfers have no distinct planes in their swings at all, swinging in a constantly changing loop of directions. In general (although not always true), the less complex or out-of-plane a golfer's clubhead path motion, the more consistently they will execute solid and repeatable swings, and the higher their percentage of "solid" golf shots.

As club length changes, it forces the swing plane angle of a golfer to change, as seen for my driver and wedge swings in Figure 2.1.4.2. Longer clubs require flatter (lower angle) swing planes, while shorter clubs require more upright (larger angle) swing plane angles for any given golfer.

2.1.4.2.

2.1.5 Normal swings don't work from trouble

Understand, golfers set-up and make their normal swings from good lies on level terrain most of the time. No matter how good their normal swing is, however, it won't always help them get out of trouble because they can't use it when they're in trouble (because of different stances, different postures and stuff around the ball).

2.1.5.1.

While their normal set-ups and swings may not be perfect, golfers groove them on practice ranges and in everyday play. They develop sub-conscious compensations to adjust for their deficiencies, and incorporate them into their normal swings. Their compensating swings are the "heart" of their normal games.

An example of how a set-up deficiency can cause trouble, however, can be seen when a golfer normally positions his ball too far forward in his stance. From good lies in the fairway he can learn to "chase-after" the ball, and hit reasonable shots (Figure 2.1.5.1).

Notice the dip of Eddie's head (some golfers also employ a late hold-and-release wrist cock) through impact, as he demonstrates the "chase" move in this figure. Depending on how much they practice it, golfers can get reasonably proficient at hitting shots from level lies with a chase swing.

A chase swing ultimately limits a player's game, however, because it becomes difficult to execute on sloping terrain lies and under pressure (when hand and wrist muscles get tense, and swing timing gets too fast). Watch Eddie's chase swing try to hit a ball from a severe downhill lie. With that same set-up error (ball too far forward), the chase swing can produce a "flub" (Figure 2.1.5.2) of epic proportions.

Who knows where this ball will go? For sure, it probably won't fly dead to the target with good trajectory and backspin, as originally intended.

2.1.5.2.

Modern courses present difficult situations. Every time a golfer changes away from his normal set-up posture, putting his muscles, bones and joints into different relative positions, his swing must undergo significant changes. Look at the obviously different set-up positions Ken Venturi gets into for shots from greenside moguls in Figure 2.1.5.3 (moguls by architect Pete Dye, TPC Sawgrass, Ponte Vedra, Florida). Just imagine the different swings and swing feels he has to make to successfully execute from these different set-ups.

2.1.5.3.

Trouble lies require special set-ups. Golfers produce their normal shot-patterns around their targets from perfect lies on level fairways. Add to this a non-level stance on uneven ground, and the quality of their swing degrades, causing the spread of their shot-pattern to grow significantly. Then add additional trouble (stuff) around the ball which gets in the way (grass clumps, weeds, roots or tree limbs) of their backswing or downswing as their club approaches the ball. At this point where their shots will go becomes anybody's guess.

This is why normal swings, even the best normal swings, often won't work from trouble. Trouble lie interference can cause bad swing planes, shot contact away from the sweet-spot, or even foreign substances coming between the club face and ball at impact. Attempts to compensate for unique lies, stances and set-up positions, with never-before-practiced swing plane adjustments, lead to shot-patterns which expand exponentially ... often to disastrous proportions!

2.1.5.3.

A number of trouble shots probably look easy when you see them played from the proper Damage Control set-up, by the world's best players on TV. They look like simple swings, the players escape with no penalty and save par, and you are convinced to try the same shot the next time you find yourself in similar trouble.

The problem is, 1) you didn't notice the set-up change the pro made before executing his escape swing, and 2) you don't have a feel for how to make the swing, turn through the shot, or keep your balance. There is a chance you've never practiced such a shot, never even once in your life.

If you try this shot with no change in your normal set-up or swing, aim at the pin and let fly, you very possibly could unleash a badly off-line shot which flies out of the frying pan ... into the fire. One more poor swing and you will have the disaster hole that ruins your round.

I hope this picture of a "normal" swing, and what happens to it in trouble, is clear to you. A normal swing from a normal set-up:

      a) Is not a circle
      b) Has a wider backswing than downswing arc behind you
      c) Has an arc bottom occurring just forward of the middle of the stance
      d) Should move the club head in a swing plane which passes through the ball, your sternum and shoulder line at address

From trouble lies however, the normal swing thoughts, keys, feel or balance don't produce their normal results, because so often you can't make normal swings from non-normal body positions. To see why this is true, let's look at how changing your set-up in terms of spine positions, stance-width and ball position affects your swing and shot results. In other words, let's look at some set-up-ology.

2.2   Spine Angles Influence Swing Mechanics

Spine angles are the angles of your spine (relative to your lower body, the ground, or your swing plane) in the direction perpendicular to your shot direction. In other words, when you bend over closer to the ball or stand up straighter farther from the ball, your spine angle changes.

While your posture may have been of passing interest to you in the past, to play with Damage Control you need to understand how the position of your spine affects your ability to swing. Spine angle is fundamental to Damage Control. Because how you set-up and position your body before your swing is critical to your swing performance in trouble.

2.2.1 Your spine-to-swing plane angle affects the natural efficiency of your swing

The power of a golf swing is similar - yet different from a baseball swing. For both swings power is more natural and easier to generate when the club head (or bat) swings perpendicular to the spine, than when they do not. In this way they are similar (Figure 2.2.1.1). This power dependency shows maximum and fairly consistent power around the perpendicular (90-degree) angle, but power decreases dramatically as the swing plane moves farther away from perpendicular. The swings differ in that baseball swings are usually closer to being perpendicular to the spine than golf swings (except when baseballers go after bad pitches). This is because golfers play with a ball on the ground, while baseballs usually come to batters somewhere up between their shoulders and knees.

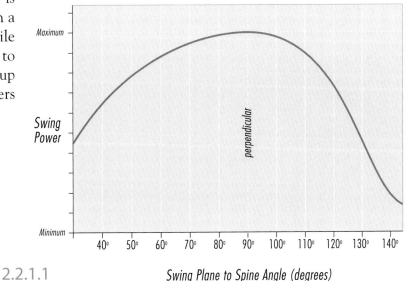

2.2.1.1   Swing Plane to Spine Angle (degrees)

If you don't understand this, grab a golf club or a bat and make some swings as in Figure 2.2.1.2. In either game, as the club head (or bat) swings farther above or below the spine - the swing gets more difficult to make and less powerful.

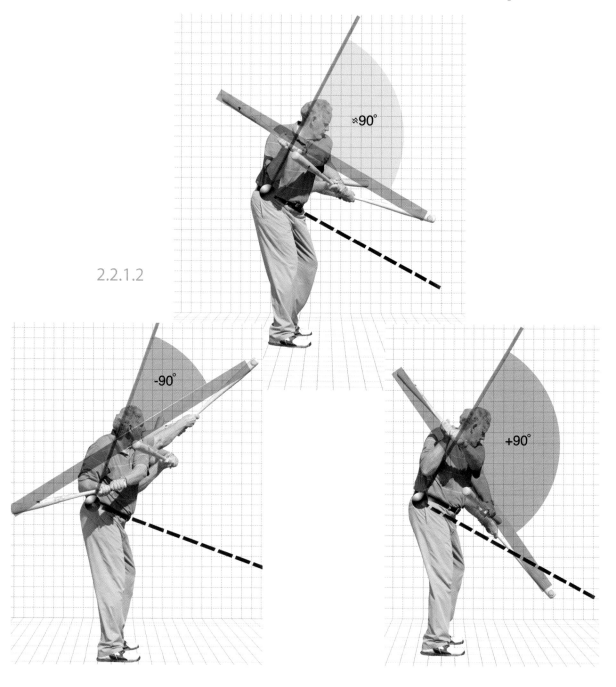

2.2.1.2

2.2.2 Bending over or standing up affects spine-to ground-angle

Your spine-to-ground angle is measured (looking downline from behind) as the angle between your spine and the ground. It can be made smaller by bending over closer to the ball, or increased by standing up straighter, moving your spine into a more vertical position (Figure 2.2.2.1).

2.2.2.1

On level ground, the more vertical the spine the easier it is to make flatter swings, all other things being equal. As you can see, when a golfer stands upright with his spine nearly vertical, it's easy to swing in a more horizontal (flatter) swing plane. When he bends over, putting his spine in a more horizontal position the opposite is true. In this case the vertical swing becomes the easier to make (Figure 2.2.2.2).

2.2.2.2

Applying this principle to a shot under tree limbs, it's better to make a flat swing from "on-your-knees" (spine more vertical), than from a standing bent over position (Figure 2.2.2.3ab).

2.2.2.3

A golfer's spine-to-ground angle , height, arm, and club length all influence his swing plane. The shorter you are and the longer your arms and clubs, the more upright you will stand and the flatter you will swing (Figure 2.2.2.4).

Upright swings require the opposite spine-to ground angle relationship, as compared to flat swings. Bending over encourages a more horizontal spine, and makes swinging a club vertically much easier. It also helps to use the shortest club with which you can accomplish the shot (Figures 2.2.2.5 and 2.2.2.6) in making upright swings.

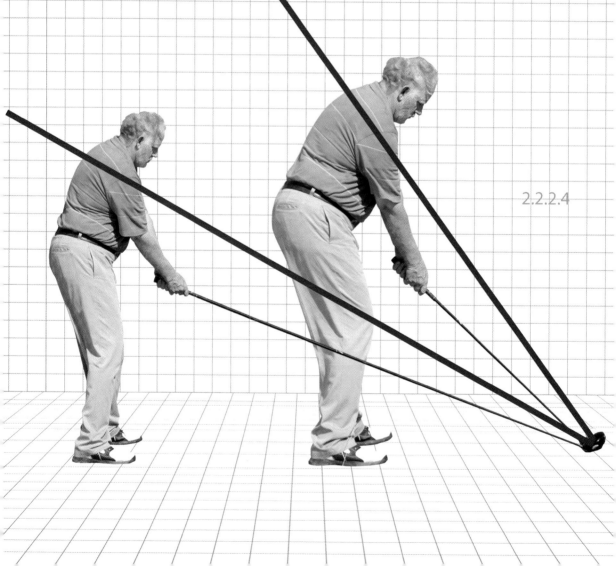

2.2.2.4

2.2.2.6.

2.2.3 Spine-to-trunk angle affects hip rotation

The spine-to-trunk angle is the angle between the spine and lower body (hips and thighs), as seen looking downline from behind a golfer. The closer to 180-degrees or a straight line this angle becomes, the easier and more powerfully the lower body can be rotated. Conversely, the more bent-over a golfer stands, making this angle smaller, the more difficulty they encounter in rotating their hips and lower body.

Even when the spine is upright, the hips are still difficult to rotate if the spine-to-trunk angle is small. Such a position is required if you must hit a shot from under a tree limb (Figure 2.2.3.1). If you don't believe this, try rotating your hips while swinging from a deep-squat position, sitting in a chair, or sitting on the ground .

2.2.3.1

2.2.4 Take your spine angles to the mirror.

Now lay this book down, stand in front of a mirror, and internalize these three fundamentals of set-up-ology.

1) Standing up = vertical spine = flat swing. All other things being equal, the more vertically you position your spine, the flatter (more horizontal) your swing plane will become. Set up as you normally do for a "normal" swing with any club and watch yourself swing in a mirror. Notice the angle of your swing plane (relative to the floor). Then stand up a little more vertically, imagine a ball on the side of a hill about a foot above your feet, and swing again. Notice your swing plane getting flatter. Finally, stand perfectly straight up, imagine your ball in a tree at shoulder height, and see how easily and powerfully you can swing at it in a flat, almost horizontal swing plane (Figure 2.2.4.1).

2.2.4.1

2) Bending over = horizontal spine = upright swing. The more horizontal your spine, the more naturally upright (vertical) your swing plane will become. Start again from your "normal" address position and watch yourself swing in the mirror. As you bend over more, getting your spine closer to horizontal, your swing plane motion will become more upright (Figure 2.2.4.2).

2.2.4.2

3) Squat = locked hips = minimum power. The smaller the angle between your spine and trunk, the more difficult it will be to rotate your lower body during a swing, and the more upper body power you must rely on in these conditions. To feel this, start from your normal address posture and swing in a flat swing plane with your eyes closed, concentrating on how easy and natural the swing feels. Then, keeping your spine-to-ground angle constant, squat lower to decrease your spine-to-trunk angle and swing again. Feel if making the swing is easier or more difficult. Squat down even lower (making your spine-to-trunk angle even smaller) and repeat the same swing. Feel how much more restricted your hips feel, and how much less powerful your swing feels. Notice how much more effort it takes to rotate your lower body and make a full swing back and through (Figure 2.2.4.3). Now take the final step and sit on the ground. This will be your smallest spine-to-trunk angle, and will surely create your most difficult lower-body rotation position, and least powerful swing.

2.2.4.3

2.3 Spine Tilt vs. Lean

Spine tilt and spine lean refer to moving your spine forward or back toward or away from your target (parallel to the target line direction). This is opposite to your other spine angles which change as you bend over more or stand up straighter (moving perpendicular to the target line). Spine tilt is the side-to-side tilting of your spine toward or away from the target relative to the centerline of your lower body, as seen from a face-on view (Figure 2.3.0.1). There should be very little or no spine tilt in your normal set up for shots with good lies on level terrain.

Spine lean occurs when a golfer leans his entire body toward or back along the target line, while maintaining zero spine tilt (Figure 2.3.0.2).

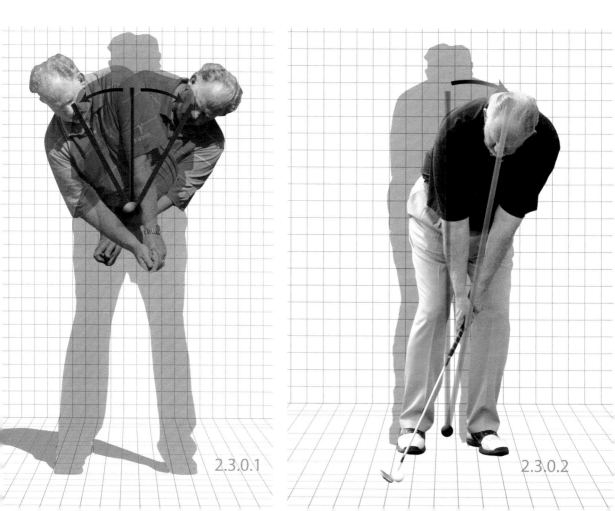

2.3.0.1   2.3.0.2

Either spine tilt or lean can change the angle of a golfer's spine relative to the ground, and affect how his swing arc encounters whatever the ball is sitting on. See this in Figure 2.3.0.3, where the downswing arcs for both a forward and backward spine tilt descend too steeply into the ground, sometimes hitting fat, behind the ball.

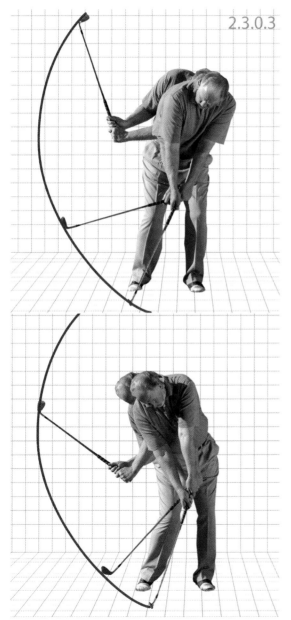

2.3.0.3

Spine tilt also creates a second problem. The farther your spine tilts away from your lower body centerline, the more difficulty you will have in rotating your lower body and swinging powerfully (Figure 2.3.0.4). So for two reasons, spine tilt is not good in posturing for a golf swing, in fact it's something to be avoided!. Most golfers do it all the time however; because it's a natural and instinctive thing to do.

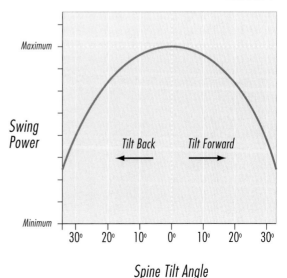

2.3.0.4

Spine Tilt Angle

2.3.1 Golfers tend to tilt back on downhill lies

Your head is heavy, and your instinct for balance always influences you to keep your spine vertically under your head and balanced above your feet. Sometimes, however, you can't hit good golf shots from a good-balance position. For example when your ball lies on a downhill slope, to keep your head in good balance you instinctively stand vertically (Figure 2.3.1.1). This positions your spine away from being perpendicular to the ground, making it more likely you'll hit the ground behind the ball.

The proper set-up for downhill slopes is to spread your stance (feet) more than normal to provide a wider base, then lean forward to get your spine closer to perpendicular to the ground. This will also place a disproportionate and unusual loading on your forward leg, knee and ankle, and make keeping your balance as you swing a real challenge.

Because this forward weight distribution is unusual doesn't mean it's wrong. In fact for downhill trouble lies, it's exactly what you need to maintain through impact, to execute a successful shot (Figure 2.3.1.2).

2.3.1.1.

2.3.1.2.

Setting your spine perpendicular to the ground is not always necessary. For small swings used for short pitch or chip shots, it may be more comfortable to use a normal (vertical spine) stance. In this case, you must play the ball back in your stance to avoid hitting the shot fat. You should be able to make clean ball contact before hitting turf if you practice this. A perfect set-up illustrating this normal-balance posture for a short pitch is shown by short game great Seve Ballesterous in Figure 2.3.1.3.

2.3.1.3.

2.3.2.1

2.3.2   Golfers tilt forward on uphill terrain

On uphill shots your instinct for good balance again wants your spine to be vertical (Figure 2.3.2.1). This is exactly opposite from what happens on downhill lies, and makes your downswing arc dig straight into the ground. Such impact can be very hard on the hands and wrists and is not conducive to good shot-making.

If, however, you take an extra-wide stance and move your spine to be perpendicular to the ground (maintain your spine-tilt = zero) as shown in Figure 2.3.2.2, you can make a good escape swing. That is, you can make a good swing "if" you can keep from falling backward as you swing the club forward through impact. This is actually difficult to execute, because most of your weight is on your back foot in this set-up, and less than normal weight transfer will move onto your forward foot through impact (because of gravity), unless you force it to do so.

2.3.3 Check your balance in the mirror

Now please lay this book down again, stand up, get a club (any club), and get in front of a mirror. You need to make some swings to see, feel, and internalize the effects spine lean and tilt can have on your swing mechanics. Consider it just another quick drill in your study of set-up-ology.

Spine tilt inhibits lower body rotation. First make a few of your normal swings from a level lie. Close your eyes and swing, focusing on the feel of your swings. Next tilt your spine forward and swing, then tilt it back and swing again. Feel the decreasing swing power you can produce as your spine tilt angle increases in either direction from zero.

Now get some object about 6-inches high, and imagine you are going to hit a shot from a downhill lie. Place your back foot up on the 6-inch object, keep your spine vertical for good balance, imagine a ball in the middle of your stance on the severe downhill slope, and swing. Are you aware you would have hit 6-inches to a foot behind the ball with that swing? (Figure 2.3.3.1A)

Next widen your stance and lean toward the target, to remove any spine tilt angle (Figure 2.3.3.1B). This gets your spine perpendicular to the ground you're standing on (and hitting from). Now swing again. See how bad this balance feels, but also feel how you would have hit the downhill shot solidly, without hitting the ground behind the ball. The key to remember here is, get your spine as nearly perpendicular to the ground (your shoulders parallel to the ground) as possible, so your spine-tilt angle will be close to zero.

Experience the uphill lie in the same way. This time put your forward foot on the 6-inch high object, and from an extra-wide stance you'll have to lean away from the target instead of toward it, to avoid a bad spine angle with the ground (Figure 2.3.3.2). Again, feel how difficult it is to keep your balance in this posture, but how much better the swing feels (relative to hitting a good shot) if you force a good body turn through impact.

Now you should be getting the feel of putting your body into position (wide stance and minimum spine tilt) to make good solid swings from sloping lies. You've become aware of another important fundamental of set-up-ology.

2.3.3.1A 2.3.3.1B

2.3.3.2

2.4 Stance Width Affects your Stability, Balance, Ability to Turn, and Power

There is no perfect stance for all golf shots. But there is a perfect stance for every individual shot. This is especially true for shots from trouble. The perfect stance is the one which balances the stability, power, and balance of the player, while making the swing the easiest to perform and create solid contact under the circumstances.

There are as many stances as there are lies, shots and players in the game. Therefore, it's essentially impossible to remember the exact perfect stance for every lie and shot. Instead, for good Damage Control, you need to learn the "principles of stance" which can then serve you for the rest of your golf career.

2.4.1 Narrow stances make turning easy, but aren't stable

Turning or rotating your body around your spine is easy when your feet are close together. You can put your feet as close together as you want and still not feel resistance to rotating your body. A very narrow stance may not be too stable, however, and won't provide a good base to push against to produce maximum power. As your feet get farther apart, you can generate more powerful swings until you get them too far apart (Figure 2.4.1.1). Also, whether your toes (feet) are turned inward toward each other (pigeon-toed) or outward (like a duck), can have an effect on how easy it is to rotate your body around your spine.

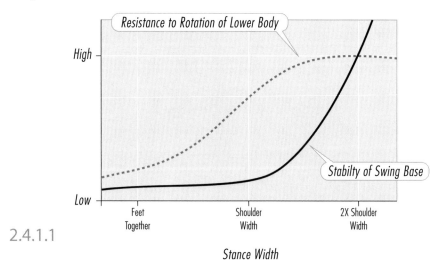

2.4.1.1

2.4.2 Wide stances are more stable, but restrict the lower body turn

Wide stances have the opposite effect from narrow stances; the wider ... the more stable. Too wide a stance, however, can limit your ability to turn your lower body, decrease your ability to generate power, and hurt your balance (by restricting knee flexibility and ability to maintain an athletic position). The general rule is: the wider the stance, the more stable the swing base and the more power you can generate, up to a certain width (see Greg Norman in Figure 2.4.2.1: very wide, stable and powerful). Most golfers prefer a stance somewhere close to - but wider than - their shoulder width for power shots. A less-than-shoulder-width stance usually feels better for short game finesse shots. Because golfers differ so much in stature and every trouble lie is different, however, there is no specific rule for stance width in all situations.

2.4.2.1

2.4.3 Internalization time again

Internalizing how your stance can influence your swing is easier to accomplish through feel, than by reading particulars in a book. For this reason I ask you to get up again, grab a club, and try the swing sequences described below in front of a mirror:

Stance narrow vs. wide: You can immediately feel the difference your stance width can make in a swing. There is no right or wrong here, no one stance is perfect or another bad. They are just different, sometimes quite different from your normal stance on level lies. The important point is, one particular stance will be best for every different trouble shot you encounter. The question then becomes, can you internalize your stance fundamentals well enough to be able to find the best stance once you are in … and trying to escape from … trouble.

Stand with your feet together and a club across your shoulders as Eddie is doing in Figure 2.4.3.1. Swing (rotate) your body around your spine. Close your eyes so your attention is tuned completely to the feel of your rotation motion. Now feel how almost your entire lower body is swinging in rhythm with your upper body, back and through, back and through, as shown. There's not much resistance to turning, but also not much of a base to generate power from.

Widen your stance in steps, and feel your lower body begins to meet resistance as your stance gets wider. Imagine and feel the base which provides good lower body resistance to coil against, and the most power.

Then keep on widening your stance and swinging. When you get your feet far enough apart, you can hardly turn your hips at all. Your swing will then be essentially all upper body: not bad, but not your most powerful.

A fundamental of set-up-ology is to get your stance into a position to allow swinging freely enough to make solid contact with the ball, keep your balance and stability through impact, all while generating enough clubhead speed to escape safely from the trouble you're in.

2.4.3.1

The feelings of stance width vs. power you have just experienced will stay with you forever. It's like riding a bicycle; once you feel it, you'll never forget it. This means when you next get into trouble, move your feet between practice swings until they feel optimized for the swing you need to get out.

2.5 Solid Contact, Ball Position and Face-Angle are Critical

Perhaps the most important part of any shot from trouble is the contact your club makes with the ball. Without proper ball position relative to your swing arc, clean contact, and the proper clubface angle through impact, your shot is not likely to escape on the trajectory or with the velocity you desire. That is ... if it escapes at all. While this may seem obvious, clean, solid contact is accomplished in surprisingly few trouble shots. It is often of no great concern to golfers before they swing at their trouble shot.

2.5.1 Impact conditions are critical

When a trouble lie presents something behind the ball prohibiting your normal swing from contacting the ball cleanly, you have a problem. This something behind the ball could be a clump of grass, a bulging tree root, a ridge of sand, a bush, or any number of obstacles on the course (Figure 2.5.1.1).

Your problem could even be the "big-ball", the earth. On a down-slope, with your back foot above your front foot (Figure 2.5.1.2), it is incredibly easy to hit the big green ball before you make contact with the little white one.

Even if you heed the advice offered previously in Section 2.3 (eliminate spine tilt and match your shoulders to the slope), I still recommend setting-up with the white ball a little back in your stance on downhill lies, to give yourself a safety margin against hitting the green one first.

You also need several clubs more loft to compensate for slope and the ball being back in your stance. More importantly, however, if you don't make solid contact with a trouble shot, you're not likely to enjoy the result.

It doesn't matter what prevents you from hitting the ball solidly. You must figure a way to get around, under, over, or through it, if you want to pull off a good escape shot. How to accomplish this task is what I want to discuss next.

2.5.1.1

2.5.1.2

2.5.2 Ball Position (positioning your body and swing-arc to the ball)

At the Pelz Golf Institute we define forward vs. back ball position on level terrain as: The position of the ball along your target line, relative to the center of your stance (Figure 2.5.2.1). Golfer's often ask us about where they should position their ball for this shot or that, and we can answer them precisely once we've seen them swing (on level ground).

But we can't do this for Damage Control shots, which require you to play the ball way forward in some trouble lies, and way back in others. The most important thing about ball position in any trouble shot (except in sand), is that the ball sits exactly on or behind where your swing arc will start to hit the ground (Figure 2.5.2.2A). This means no matter what stance you take, or the shape, plane or path of your swing, your club will contact the golf ball before it hits the ground, and create the cleanest contact possible.

If your ball position is forward of where your club contacts turf, however, your fat shot result will not be good (Figure 2.5.2.2B). No matter where you think you have your ball positioned, if it is wrong for the trouble swing you are preparing to make ... you're looking for disaster.

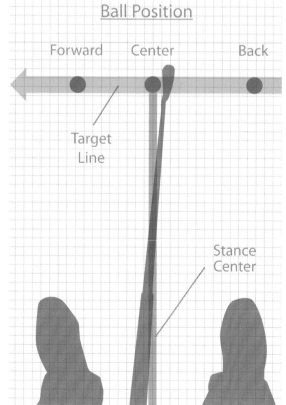

2.5.2.1

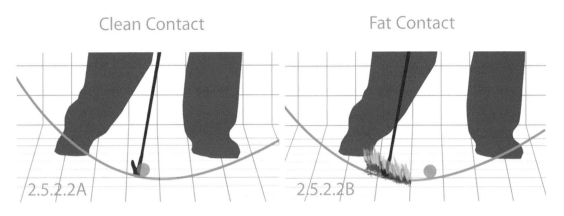

Clean Contact   Fat Contact

2.5.2.2A   2.5.2.2B

2.5.3 Verify your Divot ... before you position the ball

A fundamental of set-up-ology is to have the ball in the best possible position for the swing you're about to make, before you make it. But awkward stances on uneven terrain don't produce the same swing shapes as normal swings from level lies. Because of this, you can't know exactly where your ball should be positioned on trouble shots, until you've taken your stance and know what the shape of your swing will be

The Damage Control system to accomplish ball position is simple: verify where your club will contact the turf by making a good, realistic practice swing. Duplicate the exact same stance and set-up position you anticipate for the real shot in this practice swing. Then, look carefully and notice where the exact start of your divot occurred (Figure 2.5.3.1).

Once you see the start of your divot (the back, not the center), move into position for the shot by placing your ball exactly on or slightly behind that spot in your stance. This placement is an important fundamental of Damage Control - solid ball contact. It will save you from many disaster holes in the future.

2.5.3.1

2.5.4 Face angle influences ball flight

Many golfers have been told the golf ball starts on the path line of the club head through impact, then spins and curves from that line based on the face-angle of the club head at impact. As a result, most golfers spend their entire careers working on the path (and swing plane) of their club through the impact zone.

The truth of the matter is, the face-angle of your club has a significant influence on the direction in which your shots start to fly. You can demonstrate this to yourself on the practice tee by hitting a few shots in three different ways, as follows:

1) Down-the-line path, square face. First, set a two-by-four on edge aimed at your target to make sure the swing path of your club travels basically along the 2x4 line through impact. Hit several 7-iron shots normally, with your normal grip and clubface aimed squarely at your target at address. This should be your normal down-the-line swing path which hits your normal shots toward your target. Hit enough of them to be assured everything is behaving normally (Figure 2.5.4.1).

2) Down-the-line path, open face. Next take the same stance with your same grip position at address with the same club, but this time have the clubface of your 7-iron laid-open by about 30-degrees to the right of target (Figure 2.5.4.2) before you grip it. Double-check the club face is open when your grip is normal, then make the same swing path down the 2x4 line as you did before (when your clubface was aimed at the target). Shots fly immediately to the right because the clubface was open at impact, not because your swing path went over there!

3) Down-the-line path, closed face. Now close the clubface at address (then grip it as normal) and make some more swings along the same 2x4 swing path. See how the shots fly to the left now because of the closed clubface, even though your swing path is still along the 2x4 line (Figure 2.5.4.3)?

Understanding your clubface angle at impact influences initial shot direction can be a tremendous asset in planning and aiming escape shots from trouble. Golfers often hit shots straight into trees and other trouble, because they expect their ball to start on their swing path line.

2.5.4.1-3

2.5.5 Feel impact

You now know intellectually that clean contact, ball position and face angle are important if escape shots are to be successful. But you need to feel and internalize this importance, so you won't forget it in the heat of battle. If you will please once more get up and get a ball and a club, you can experience this feel.

2.5.5.1

Address a ball in your normal set-up position, but don't swing. Imagine smacking the ball solidly and hitting a perfect shot, with that square club face position. Now rotate the shaft with one hand without moving the other, so the clubface is open by 30-degrees while your hands stay in your normal grip position. Imagine how far right the shot would fly from a normal swing with this set-up (Figure 2.5.5.1).

Imagining where the shot will fly off the clubface is something you will want to do before every trouble shot in the future. Rotate the clubface closed now, again within your normal grip, and again imagine how far left the shot would start from this impact position. This feeling of your shot starting line relative to your clubface position, before every trouble shot, is paramount to Damage Control.

While you have a club in your hand, I want you to learn to feel something else. Turn the clubface back to square (without moving your feet) and move the ball way back in your stance (away from the target) until it is opposite your back ankle. Now address an imaginary ball as if it were up in the middle of your stance. Imagine making a perfect swing at the imaginary ball, but hitting the real ball.

Feel the shot (Figure 2.5.5.2). You might whiff the ball completely, swinging right over the top of it, or hit the top part of the ball and dribble it a few yards out in front of you. Now feel what a different swing you would have to make to hit that real ball solidly without moving your feet, when it is so far back in your stance.   This is a feel you never want before a trouble shot.

2.5.5.2

If you are ever over a shot in the future and feel you must make a swing like this to hit it - STOP! Step back and take another practice swing - change your stance, ball position, spine-angle ... do something ... to give yourself a good-solid swing feel, before you try the shot.

The point is: before every trouble shot feel you are set-up optimally to hit the shot with the easiest, most consistent, most powerful, most solid swing you could possibly muster, under the lie conditions you are in.

2.6 Set-up-ology is Fundamental to Escape Shot Success

OK. You've felt how important your set-up, posture, spine-angles, stance, solid contact, ball position, and face angle can be in the golf swing. I hope you realize; it's important to feel these are all as good as you can get them, before you swing at any trouble shot. You're going to have to be able to imagine and feel this before you can achieve Damage Control and consistently escape from trouble.

Please understand. I'm not trying to get you to swing a golf club like a baseball bat, or change your normal swing in any way. But golf's trouble shots are often played from extremely uneven terrain, the ball often sits on strange angles and levels relative to our feet, and normal swings won't work in these conditions.

We must contort our bodies, bend over, lean our spines and position the ball in new and different ways during swings from trouble, in almost every round we play. And to play with Damage Control, you need to know how any and all of these changes will affect your ability to swing and hit shots.

None of the set-ups or postures in this chapter are impossible to swing from. They are just different from the normal set-ups you practice and use from level lies. Once you learn to put your body in the best position to deal with the trouble lies you encounter, and practice making such swings, you can execute them quite well.

That's all for now on set-up-ology. You understand how set-up and posture can affect your ability to swing, and you've experienced the feel of some of these changes. You'll learn more set-up-ology in Chapter 7 when you actually set-up and hit shots from different trouble lies and postures. You've also felt how changing your stance, ball position, and clubface angle affects your impact and shot starting direction.

As you develop the skills to become a Damage Control player, you will stand, bend, lean, imagine and feel impact before every escape shot attempt. You will always make a realistic practice swing and verify your ball position precisely at or behind the start of your divot, before every trouble shot. And you will always be aware of this fact: Your set-up will enable … or prohibit … your escape swing success.

Normal swings don't always work perfectly, even from perfect lies. But put golfers in trouble, with difficult stances, tall grass around their ball, and obstacles interfering with their swings, and their shot-patterns go to hell … in a hand basket.

Hitting bad shots from trouble is understandable. The rocks, trees, creek banks, tall grass, mounds, water falls and bushes which place golf courses among the most beautiful places on earth, also present severe swing difficulties to golfers who trespass into their domain.

The second skill of Damage Control is swing shaping. This skill allows golfers to change the shape of their swing, and hit screaming shots from trouble lies with "Tour-Pro" consistency! Whether it's changing the radius of your backswing, making your swing plane flater, or creating a unique spine angle to the ground, shaping your swing to make solid contact with the ball is paramount to escaping from trouble.

The guiding fundamental of swing shaping is: When your normal swing won't get

3.1 Changing the Shape of your Swing

In the last chapter you saw how to set-up and position your body to make swinging from trouble lies easier. Now it's time to learn to make effective swings that will extricate balls from that trouble effectively.

The size, circularity and symmetry of your swing can be changed in many ways. Changing the timing of your wrist cock changes the position of your clubhead along its swing path. Gripping down on the shaft changes the radius of your swing path, and you can lengthen or shorten your backswing or follow through.

While these swing changes sound easy to make, they're not easy, or repeatable, if you first try to make them during actual shots on the course. In fact just the opposite is true. Most golfers have never thought of changing the shape of their swing in these ways, or how it feels to do so. And they've certainly never practiced doing it.

When in trouble, golfers recognize their club shaft must miss the tree behind the ball, but they don't know the set-up-ology to make it happen. So they swing, trying to change the club path with only their hand and wrist muscles, just hoping to miss the tree. All too often this creates a bad swing, a tree collision, and a (bad) shot which flys out of the frying pan ... into the fire.

3.1.1 Tight quarters behind

When there's not enough room behind the ball to take a normal backswing, a good swing can still be made. This kind of trouble comes in many forms, and in various severities.

Bushes, trees and fences are often culprits. Take for example when a bush allows not quite enough room for a normal backswing, by only a few inches (Figure 3.1.1.1). You can still hit this shot using an almost normal swing by playing the ball farther back in your stance . You simply move your body and swing forward to create extra space. You'll also have to close the clubface slightly to keep the ball from launching right of target, and use more loft to compensate for this closed face.

3.1.1.1 - The problem: bush behind the ball.

Normal ball position

Ball back position

Another way to combat trouble from behind is to grip down on the club. This decreases the radius of your swing, and the room you need behind the ball, by as many inches as you grip down (Figure 3.1.1.2). Of course the shorter the club, the less powerful the swing, so gripped-down shots will not fly as far as normal.

3.1.1.2

As trouble closes in even tighter behind, more extreme changes must be made to create swings to extricate the ball. Look at my situation in Figure 3.1.1.3, where my clubhead hits a tree shortly after take-away. I don't have nearly enough room if I cock my wrists gradually, as I normally do in the backswing.

3.1.1.3

1) Pre-Cock (lift club vertical)   2) Take backswing   3) Check clearance

By fully cocking my wrists before take-away (pre-cock), then keeping them fully cocked through the rest of my backswing, a normal down swing fits just inside the tree trunk (Figures 3.1.1.4 and 3.1.1.5). This shot is not as dangerous as it looks (the downswing is exactly the same as normal), but it takes practice to get used to the feel of taking a backswing with completely cocked wrists. It's a confidence thing: Cock your wrists, make a good backswing, then swing normally down and through from there.

3.1.1.5

3.1.1.6

When trouble is closer still, a different change can allow you to hit a shot. With a fence providing absolutely no room for a backswing (Figure 3.1.1.6), a shot can still be played toward a green off to the left. Set-up with your body and swing aimed down the fence line (top left photo), well right of the green. Then close the clubface to the left (top right photo). Use lots of extra loft, and take a normal swing down the fence line. After trying a few of these shots with different clubs, you'll quickly see how low, left, and far the shots fly. You'll also see how little backspin they have and how far they roll. With practice you'll learn when (and when not) to use this swing technique.

3.1.2 Obstacles and trouble ahead

When a normal set-up causes your clubhead or shaft to hit trouble after impact, you've got obstacles and trouble ahead. If by simply aiming left or right you can solve the problem, that's easy. When neither of these is an option, changing your swing shape is the only answer.

To stop your club after impact sounds easy, but it's actually difficult to do. To hit a ball hard, and then stop your hands, arms, clubhead and follow-through, almost always takes more time and room than golfers expect. This scenario often ends up bending or breaking the shaft, or hurting the golfer's hands and wrists. It's especially difficult in the heat of the moment when a golfer wants to hit an important shot to save a stroke and win a hole.

The hit-and-stop technique will work if you have enough room. The general guideline is: never hit a full strength shot if you don't have room to make at least half your normal follow-through (Figure 3.1.2.1). Even following this guideline, stopping in time takes practice and good hand coordination.

3.1.2.1

Faced with a more serious follow-through problem posed by a solid rock in front of your ball, you need to stop your club quickly after impact (Figure 3.1.2.2). With proper set-up-ology you can use the earth to stop your club, as I demonstrate in Figure 3.1.2.3 (next page). I'm warning you however, DO NOT try this swing or shot without going through the proper instruction (sidebar below) and backyard practice (detailed in Chapter 7) to develop the set-up, knowledge and swing skill to pull it off without hurting yourself!

Warning: TRY THIS SHOT ONLY AT YOUR OWN RISK.

This shot can be dangerous. It can create hand and wrist injury, break a club, splinter a shaft, or the ball can come back and hit you.

If you insist on learning this shot (at your own risk), sneak up on it in stages: first try stopping your club with NOTHING out in front of your ball. After you learn how quickly you can stop your club and how high you can launch the ball, try the shot with a soft ball over a soft obstacle such as a sponge (see Chapter 7). Only play with solids (real ball, real rock) after you are experienced and know you can hit the shot safely.

Again I warn you: Be careful ... TRY ONLY AT YOUR OWN RISK

3.1.2.2

3.1.2.3

Set-up with the ball 12-inches farther back in your stance than normal (see normal footprints in grass, Figure 3.1.2.3) and lean sharply forward. Use a club with lots of extra loft to compensate for both set-up changes. Then swing severely down into the ground and lighten your grip at impact (almost let go of the club, to protect your hands and wrists). Let the ground stop your club.

3.1.3 Trouble on the toe or heel side of your ball

When your ball decides to snuggle-up along side trouble, you must focus on making a swing to: a) Maximize contact with the ball; b) Minimize contact with the trouble; and c) Optimize the tolerance for shot-pattern scatter. In many cases perfect contact is not an option; you simply have to do the best you can and allow for the consequences in shot reaction. Many different items can cause trouble: rough grass, bushes, rocks, tree roots, even the edge of a low-lipped sand bunker. Such problems can require differing solutions, depending on which side of the ball they are on, where they lie relative to your target direction, and how hard (solid) they are (Figure 3.1.3.1).

3.1.3.1

The figures on the next 6 pages illustrate a number of trouble scenarios which can occur off first the toe, then the heel side of a club. Don't try to memorize how to play from any of these situations. Study each trouble circumstance until you understand the instruction on how it should be handled, then move to the next example. By the time you finish this section, you'll comprehend the principles of avoidance embodied in this aspect of Damage Control.

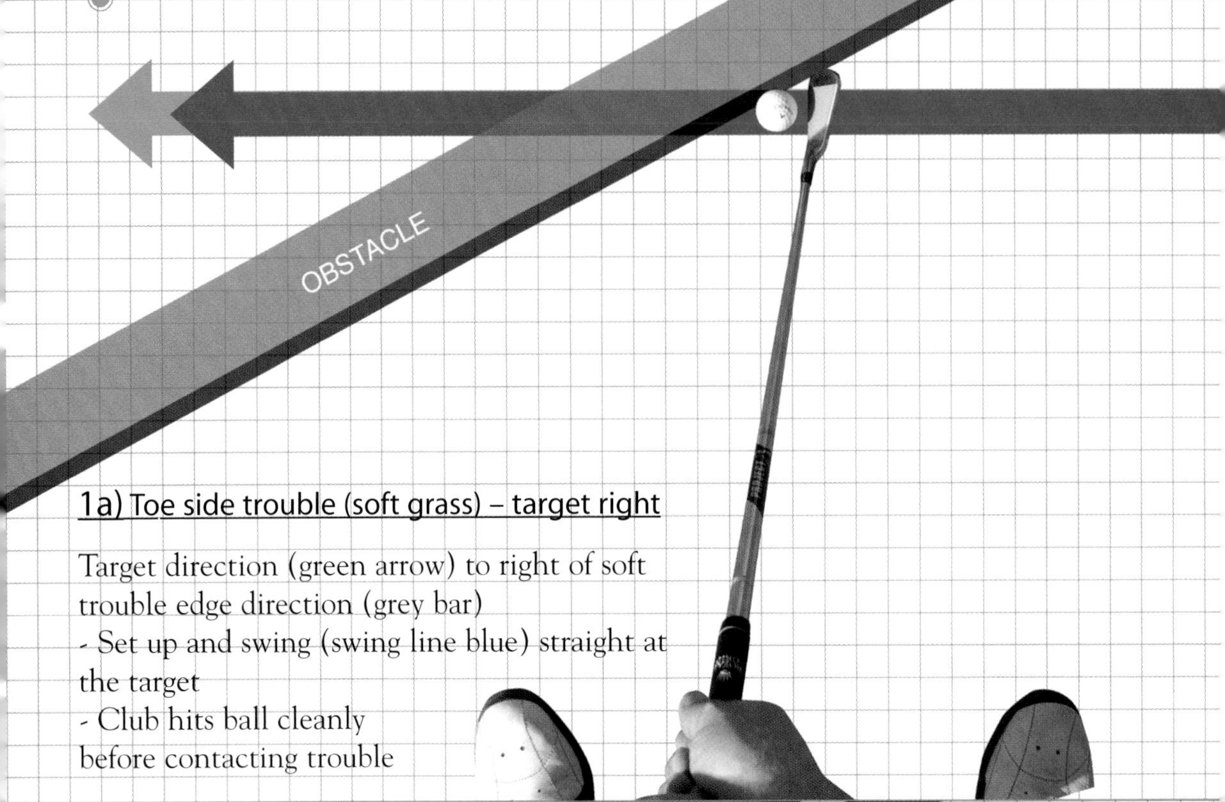

OBSTACLE

1a) Toe side trouble (soft grass) – target right

Target direction (green arrow) to right of soft trouble edge direction (grey bar)
- Set up and swing (swing line blue) straight at the target
- Club hits ball cleanly before contacting trouble

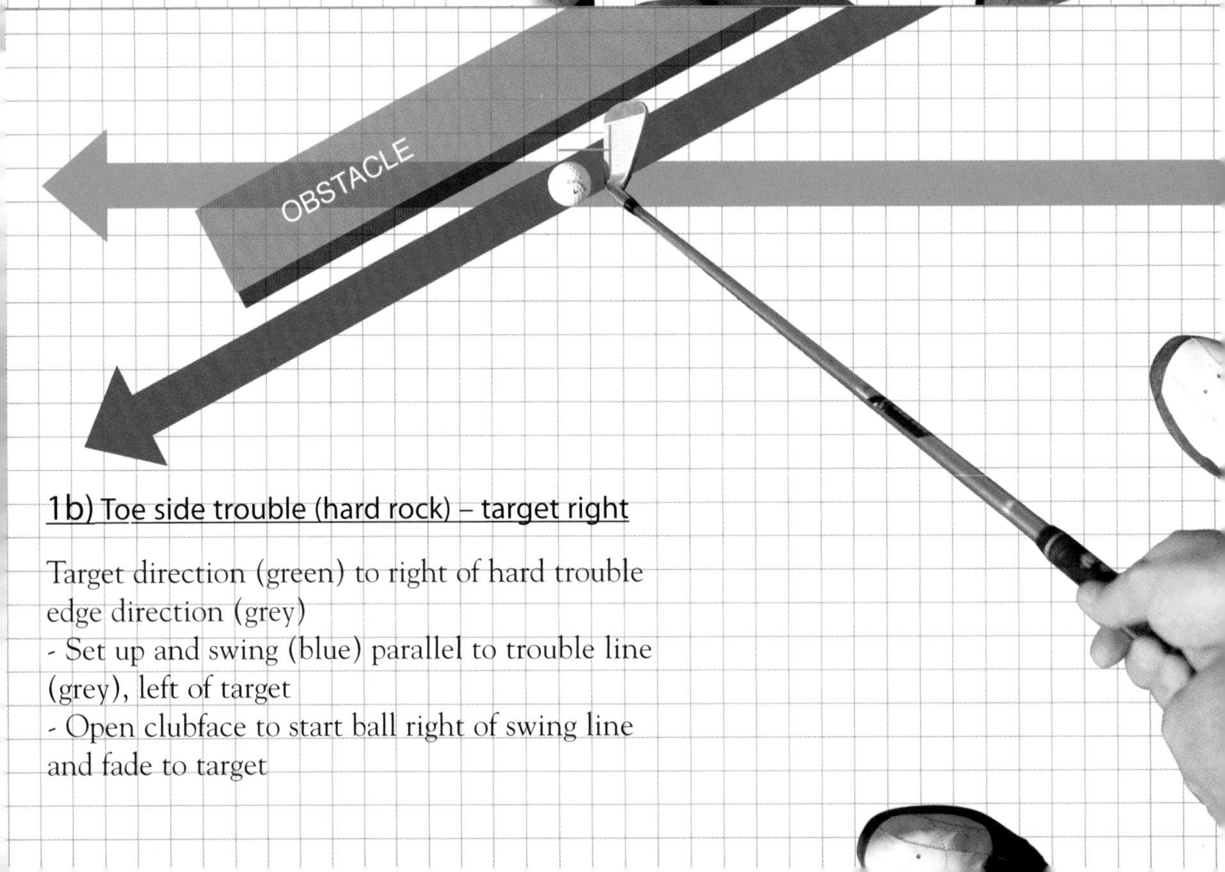

OBSTACLE

1b) Toe side trouble (hard rock) – target right

Target direction (green) to right of hard trouble edge direction (grey)
- Set up and swing (blue) parallel to trouble line (grey), left of target
- Open clubface to start ball right of swing line and fade to target

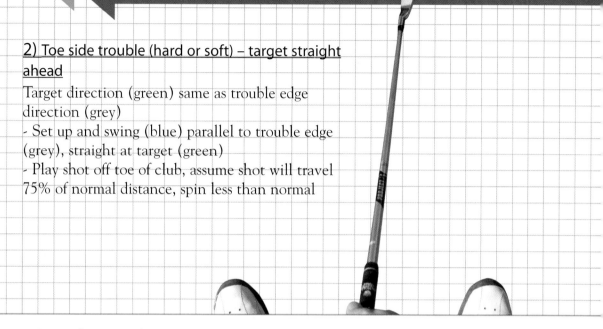

OBSTACLE

2) Toe side trouble (hard or soft) – target straight ahead

Target direction (green) same as trouble edge direction (grey)
- Set up and swing (blue) parallel to trouble edge (grey), straight at target (green)
- Play shot off toe of club, assume shot will travel 75% of normal distance, spin less than normal

NOTE: The grey bar simulates the problem obstacle, which could be "soft" like grass, meaning you could hit into or through it without hurting yourself, or "hard" like a rock, meaning hitting it would cause injury

3a) Toe side trouble (soft or hard) – target left

Target direction (green) left of trouble edge
direction (grey)
- Don't aim straight at target and try to power
through trouble before hitting ball
- Even when trouble is soft, this seldom produces
good shots

OBSTACLE

3b) Toe side trouble (soft or hard) – target left

This set-up will allow you to
hit a solid shot without ever
touching the trouble. If you
get the clubface angle
correct, the ball will start to
the left of your swing line
with some hook spin, and
draw to your target

OBSTACLE

Target direction (green) left of trouble edge
direction (grey)
- Set up and swing (blue) parallel to trouble edge
(grey)
- Close clubface to start ball left of swing line
and hook to target
- Use extra loft to compensate for closed face

4a) Heel side trouble (soft or hard) – target right

OBSTACLE

Target direction (green) right of trouble edge direction (grey)
- Don't set up directly at target and try to swing through the trouble
- Even if the trouble is only tall grass, it will affect your clubface and shot trajectory
- This technique usually does not turn out well

4b) Heel side trouble (soft or hard) – target right

If your ball is so close to a hard surface you might shank the shot, either take an unplayable lie, or try to hit the shot with a left handed swing (see Chapter 7: opposite-way swings).

OBSTACLE

Target direction (green) right of trouble edge direction (grey)
- Set up parallel to trouble edge and swing (blue) parallel to trouble edge (grey)
- Open clubface to start ball right of swing line and slice to target
- Use less loft to compensate for open face

5a) Heel side trouble (soft or hard) – target straight ahead

OBSTACLE

Target direction (green) straight ahead of trouble
edge direction (grey)
- Do not set-up and swing directly at target
unless you have plenty of room between the club
heel and trouble
- If the heel of your club hits the hard trouble
you have disaster

5b) Heel side trouble (soft) – target straight ahead

Note: You want to make absolutely sure you don't hit the ball off the club hosel. This technique
gives you a margin so you'll never hit the dreaded hosel shot from this lie. If the trouble is too
hard to hit into however, you might try a left-handed swing.

OBSTACLE

Target direction (green) straight ahead of trouble edge
direction (grey)
- Set up "slightly" left of trouble edge and swing (blue)
"slightly" into trouble (grey) after impacting ball
- Open clubface "slightly" to start ball "slightly" right of
swing line and fade to target
- Use "slightly" less loft to compensate for open face

6a) Heel side trouble (soft) – target left

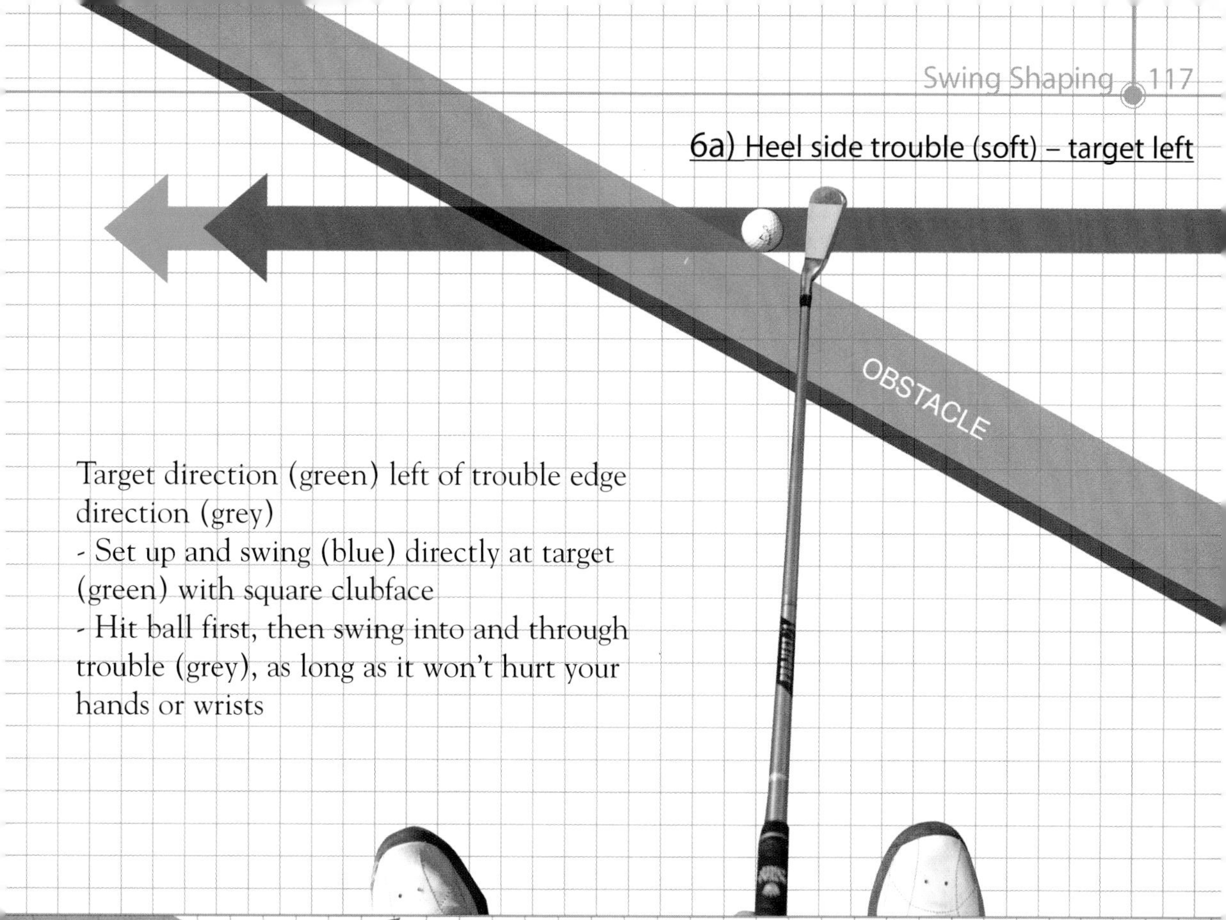

Target direction (green) left of trouble edge direction (grey)
- Set up and swing (blue) directly at target (green) with square clubface
- Hit ball first, then swing into and through trouble (grey), as long as it won't hurt your hands or wrists

OBSTACLE

6b) Heel side trouble (hard) – target left

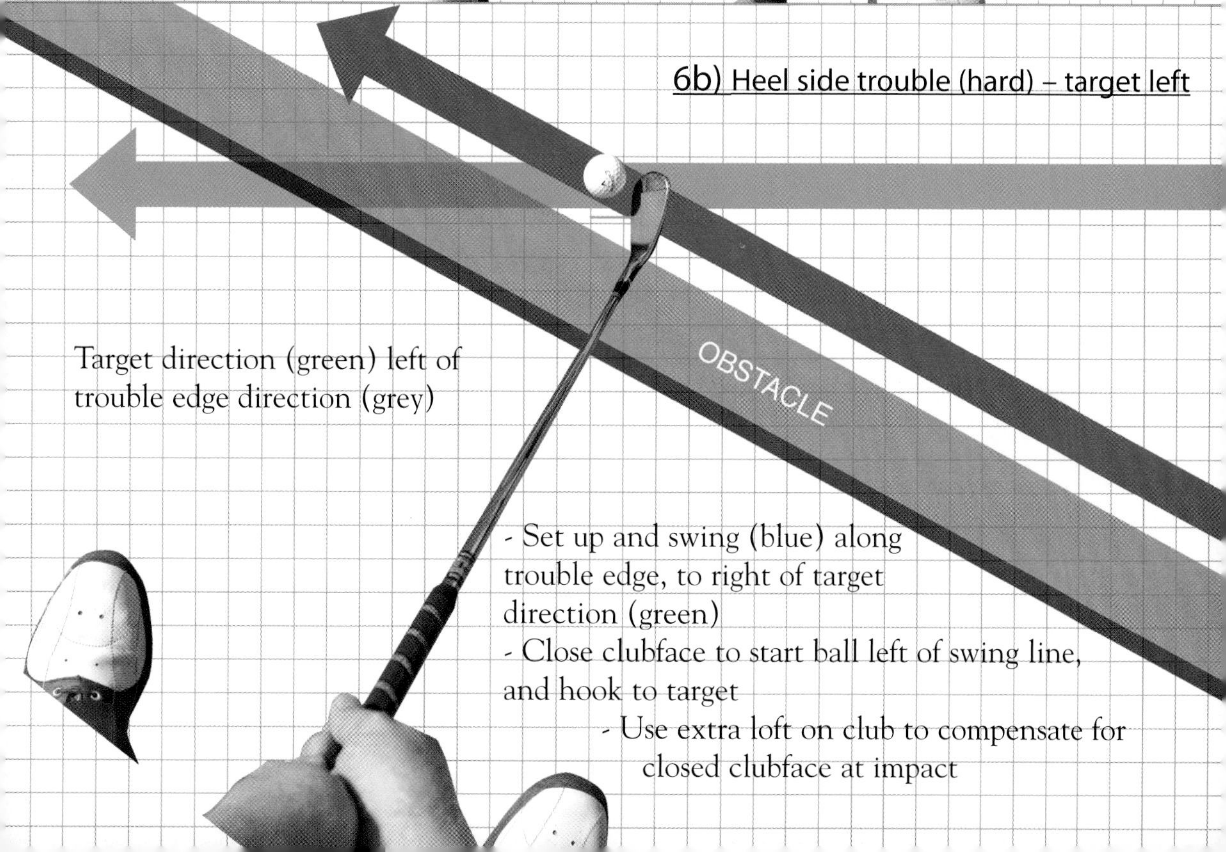

Target direction (green) left of trouble edge direction (grey)

OBSTACLE

- Set up and swing (blue) along trouble edge, to right of target direction (green)
- Close clubface to start ball left of swing line, and hook to target
- Use extra loft on club to compensate for closed clubface at impact

When grass is everywhere around the ball, and there is no way to avoid it, you've got to get your club into and out of it as quickly as you can. From really tall grass, your goal should be to use a compact and powerful swing with the shortest club you can possibly use, which still provides enough power to get through the grass and power the ball out. The tighter the swing radius, the less grass you have to swing through.

As you can see in Figure 3.1.3.4, I'm gripping down about 3-inches on my wedge, and have the face slightly open to help the club slide through the grass with less resistance. I'm also using a high lofted wedge to get the ball up and out of the grass as quickly as possible. Remember, the lower this shot launches, the more grass the ball has to pass through, and that means more power you must provide.

3.1.3.4

3.1.4 The Concept of Avoidance

It's better to avoid hitting things other than the ball, be it with your arms, shaft or clubhead. Save all the swing energy you can for the ball. No matter if trouble is in front of, beside or behind the ball; try not to hit it. That's the purpose of swing shaping: to hit the ball without hitting other things. If you absolutely can't avoid hitting them, avoid it for as long as you can, at least until after you've made contact with the ball.

When hitting obstacles is unavoidable, it's better for your follow through to swing into them, than for your down swing to pass through them. Any time your club contacts trouble before it gets to the ball, your odds of getting a perfect face angle, sweet-spot contact, and accelerating velocity through impact are degraded, while your chances of moving the ball from out of the frying pan … into the fire, are greatly enhanced. Hitting a tree limb in your backswing is much worse than hitting it at the end of your follow through, when it won't affect your shot (although it may bend your shaft).

Give yourself a margin for swing error. It's better to play shots intentionally off the toe of your club to avoid contacting a tree root, than to try to execute a perfect swing and just barely miss the root with no margin for error. Understand; human instincts are strong, and deeply ingrained. If your subconscious thinks you might hit a tree root or rock in your swing, it might flinch-away at the last moment, and result in a poor shot. It's better to plan for toe impact and get it, than to expect a solid shot but get one off the toe of a flinching clubhead.

3.2 Changing the Swing Plane

There are right and wrong ways to change the plane of your swing. Unfortunately for golfers, the most natural and intuitive way is often the wrong way.

Left to their natural instincts, golfers in trouble situations usually set-up normally, then use their hands and arms to swing weakly into more upright or flat swing planes in an attempt to miss it. Such swings are usually inconsistent, don't hit shots solidly, and frequently produce awful results. A better way to make off-plane swings is to change the initial set-up position of your body, then emphasize good upper or lower body rotation to produce strong and solid swing power.

Please note: using the combination of a proper set-up and good body rotation when in trouble often relegates the hands and arms to a function of holding-on, as in the normal golf swing. This is a good thing, as it produces results more likely to be accurate and powerful, with a higher percentage of solid shots.

3.2.1 A swing plane fundamental some golfers don't understand

Two principles of the golf swing escape the attention of many golfers. The faster and harder a golfer swings, the more strongly centripetal forces; 1) pull their swing into a plane perpendicular to their spine; and 2) pull their hands into that swing plane through impact.

These principles align with the following result: the most powerful swings most golfers make come close to a plane perpendicular to their spines. Examples of this can be seen in the driver swings of some of the powerful (only kidding in my case, but Charles Howell and Phil Mickelson hit it pretty well) driver swings of the game (Figure 3.2.1.1). While this position is not always possible to achieve from trouble, the closer you can get to it the more powerful and stable those swings will be.

3.2.1.1

3.2.1.2

A natural consequence of this is the opposite effect; the farther your swing plane moves away from the perpendicular to your spine, the less powerful or repeatable your swing will be. You can see this in the funky-weak swing I'm making after my ball got stuck up in a tree (Figure 3.2.1.2, a swing plane nowhere near my spine perpendicular).

It is important for good Damage Control, to position your body to make swings in a plane as nearly perpendicular to your spine as possible. This may mean contorting your body at address into strange positions, and emphasizing your upper-body shoulder turn to produce a higher percentage of power than normal. But if this is what it takes to produce consistent escape swings from trouble situations, you need to learn to do it

3.2.2 How to create flat vs. upright swings

In Chapter 2 you saw how setting-up with your spine-angle more vertical makes swinging in a flat plane easier, while a horizontal spine makes swinging in an upright plane easier. It was also discussed how the spine-lean, spine-to-trunk angle, and stance width of a golfer's set-up affect their ability to rotate their upper and lower bodies. I'm sure you believe these correlations, but I want to show you how they work in shaping swings on the golf course too.

Let's start by looking at what happened to Eddie when he hit his drive off to the right in the rough on a par-5 hole (Figure 3.2.2.1A). All he needs to do is punch the ball about 100-yards back into and down the fairway to make saving his par routine. From his normal posture, however, it's clear he can't hit his ball solidly. Several tree limbs will surely deflect the clubhead as he moves into impact and disrupt the shot badly.

3.2.2.1A

3.2.2.1B

If he instinctively bends over and lowers his hands to get the club shaft low enough to miss the tree limbs (Figure 3.2.2.1B), he puts himself into an even worse posture to swing from. Any shoulder rotation from this position would produce a very upright swing, so he must use his hands and wrists alone to keep the clubhead swinging below the branches. He cannot possibly generate significant power by swinging the club from this position.

The better solution (while not instinctive or natural) is to get all the way down onto his knees (Figure 3.2.2.1C) From this position his hands, shoulders, clubhead and ball all get closer to being in the same plane, and he can generate some real clubhead speed and power through impact. Also notice Eddie's spine-angle is more vertical, so he can make a more natural shoulder turn to generate a flat swing through impact without touching the limbs. Remember, the key to power and solid ball contact is getting into the position to make a good in-plane swing with good upper body rotation vs. a hands-only power swing from a bent-over set-up posture.

You should also notice Eddie changed clubs when he went to his knees. By using his utility club (which has a smaller heel and exposes no hosel to the ball) he eliminated the possibility of hitting the ball off the hosel of an iron club. Also be aware, whenever you achieve a low swing plane angle with the ground it becomes easy to catch the clubhead heel on the ground, flipping the clubface over and flubbing the shot. With a little practice in keeping the clubhead just brushing the ground, however, and not digging into it, the flip-over flub can be avoided.

3.2.2.2A   3.2.2.2B

Exactly the opposite solution works best when you need to make truly upright swings (Figure 3.2.2.2A). In this case you need to move closer, bend over more to position your spine horizontally and grip down. Then, work hard to get your shoulders to rotate from that position (Figure 3.2.2.2B). Although you'll never generate as much power from upright swings (as from flat swings), they are invaluable when in tight situations between trees.

As you can see in Figure 3.2.2.2C, even when the hips and lower body can't turn effectively (my horizontal spine and small spine-trunk angle restricted my lower body turn), decent upper body rotation can be maintained. When a good swing plane of shoulders, clubhead and ball can be achieved, adequate power can still be generated in the shot.

3.2.2.2C

3.2.3.1

3.2.3 Backhand swings can make difficult shots easier

When your ball is well above your feet (Figure 3.2.3.1), a normal swing is not easy to execute without hitting behind the ball, or hitting it way left. In this case, you need the back-handed shot. It's not that difficult to execute, but it feels strange the first time you try it.

The back-hand swing allows a good stance in this situation. Keep your shoulder anchored with your free hand to provide a stable anchor point for your swing. Play the ball out in front of your feet to contact it cleanly before scuffing the turf (Figure 3.2.3.2). You'll need to try a number of back-hand shots before you can feel the direction balls come off your clubface and how much loft, carry and roll you'll get from this swing.

Look how easy the shot from water's edge becomes, when back-handed. With a simple 7-iron swing (instead of risking a fall into the water and an alligator encounter), I can chip this shot close enough to have a good chance to save par (Figure 3.2.3.3).

3.2.3.2

3.2.3.3

3.2.4 Swings from the opposite side can save strokes

Another stroke-saver when your ball comes to rest on the opposite side of obstacles, is to learn to swing from the opposite side (Figure 3.2.4.1). By opposite side, I mean the opposite side from which ever you normally play. Anyone can learn to swing the opposite way (up-against water, a tree, or a fence), and it's actually easier than it was learning to swing the first time (your brain already knows most of the swing principles involved).

Don't, however, think you're going to hit good shots this way at first. A little practice will go a long way toward improving the feel of your opposite swing, and its results. You have to find a clubhead that works best for your swing when turned upside-down. When I tried this for the first time, my instinct told me low lofted clubs would work best. For me the opposite was true, as higher lofted clubs allowed me to hit better shots. Please beware; the first few times you try this technique (in Chapter 7), expect awful results.

But be patient. You'll be surprised how easily this will come to you (Figure 3.2.4.2). You'll never have to play many shots, or hit perfect shots with this technique. You just have to swing well enough to get your ball out of trouble and back into the game, on the first try!

3.2.4.1   3.2.4.2

3.3 Lies on Sloping Terrain

Whenever the ball lies more than 3-inches above or below your feet in your address position, you've got trouble. I've tested this aspect of shot performance thoroughly, and measured how golfers struggle mightily on shots from side hill lies. The same is true for up and downhill lies.

Lies on sloping terrain are an important part of the game, I'm sure you've experienced many of them. The farther your shots stray from the centerlines of fairways, the greater the slopes and the more rugged the terrain they tend to come to rest on. Golf course architects design slopes and undulating terrain into their trouble areas, because they know golfers have trouble handling them (while the "garden-spot" of each fairway is usually level, providing the perfect approach to the green). There are good and valid reasons golfers have problems from these lies, and overcoming them is part of the skill of swing shaping.

Swing alterations must be made to accommodate sloping terrain by changing your stance, adjusting your ball position, and by leaning your body and spine. These alterations are fraught with balance difficulties, however, and must be made with care and determination based on experience.

3.3.1 Sidehill, ball above feet

When the ball is more than 3-inches above your feet at address, several things happen. Your spine-angle tends to become more vertical, you stand farther from the ball, the club feels heavier, and your swing plane becomes flatter than normal. The loft of your club also aims to the left (for right-handed players) of your normal alignment (Figure 3.3.1.1).

3.3.1.1

If you swing using your normal feel, your clubhead will swing through impact lower than you want it to (sometimes missing under the ball). This is because your clubhead feels heavier than during normal level-lie swings. To compensate for this effect, simply imagine the ball is slightly higher than it really is. Address the ball with your clubhead slightly above it (Figure 3.3.1.2), and actually swing trying to hit above the real ball. This technique allows you to use your normal swing feel, and still achieve solid contact with these shots.

3.3.1.2

3.3.1.3 - Ernie Els in bush on last round of British Open 2004 at Troon. Ernie went on to save par from here and almost won, losing in a playoff.

When you find your ball waist-high up in a tree or bush (Figure 3.3.1.3), this extra-heavy feel becomes a really serious issue. Many golfers swing and miss such balls completely, swinging under them by several inches. Again, I recommend using your normal swing feel, but imagine the ball is several inches above where it really is (Figure 3.3.1.4), and try hitting the imaginary ball.

3.3.1.4

As with so many of the Damage Control skills, this shot is easy once you experience the heavy-club effect, understand it, and compensate for it (Figure 3.3.1.5)

3.3.1.5

3.3.2.1

3.3.2.2

3.3.2 Sidehill, ball below feet

With a ball below your feet, stand closer to the ball and lower your body down to it (squat). If the ball is not too far below your feet, you can keep your spine-angle normal while squatting, and make a good escape swing by using only a little less lower body rotation than normal (Seve, Figure 3.3.2.1)

A common misconception in golf is from this lie (ball below feet) you should aim left of your target because the slope will send the shot to the right. This sounds good because the opposite (club loft aims left for ball above feet, Section 3.3.1 above) happens for the opposite slope direction.

The truth is, however, your clubface aim should remain essentially normal (Figure 3.3.2.2), because as you squat down with your knees to reach the ball, your shaft angle and clubface aim doesn't change much. Care must be taken in this shot to avoid catching the heel of the club in the turf (causing the clubface to flip over closed, hitting the ball left) or swing out from the body and hit a hosel shot to the right.

As the ball moves farther below your feet, you must bend over more to reach it (squatting more doesn't work because your knees get in the way). This means your swing will consist mostly of upper body power, and the club will feel lighter. Balance is key to this shot - look again at Seve – he is playing left (for increased stability) with an open clubface.

3.3.3 Downhill slope, back foot above front

From Set-up-ology (Section 2.3.1) you may remember; using normal balance makes for a bad set-up on a downhill slope. For downhill lies; widen your stance, lean forward, use more loft (to compensate for the slope), grip down on the shaft, and position the ball back in your stance.

With forward lean, more weight than normal is thrown onto your forward leg and foot, creating a difficult balance situation during the swing. To make good swings from downhill slopes put more emphasis on your upper body turn, because your lower body turn will be restricted somewhat by your wide stance. Focus on staying down-and-through the shot until you are well past impact, then release from your stance and walk through your finish (to keep from falling on your face). Especially when making powerful swings from downhill slopes, make sure you can release your body after impact and walk down the hill without stepping over or into something harmful (Figure 3.3.3.1).

You will learn your "lean-limit" doing downhill drills in Chapter 7. This is the maximum you can lean forward to get your spine more perpendicular to the ground, and still produce good swing speed. There is always danger of hitting behind balls on downhill lies, and beware these shots usually carry good distances, but fly lower and roll farther than shots from level lies.

3.3.3.1

3.3.4 Uphill slope, front foot above back

When hitting shots from uphill slopes, the golf swing gets much more difficult. From a wider than normal stance lean your shoulders to the slope (back), this time use a club with less loft to compensate for the slope, and grip down on the club shaft (Figure 3.3.4.1).

The difficulty of the shot comes from having to force your body rotation (and resultant weight transfer) to move through impact up the hill. This action takes both understanding and practice, because you must delay your worry about catching your balance until after the shot is gone (Figure 3.3.4.2).

Just as for downhill lies, you must learn your "lean-limit" for good swings. I warn you; exaggerating your body turn to produce club head acceleration past impact (which requires rotating your weight uphill through impact), is not an easy or natural thing to do. (Note: whatever you do, don't fall back until after impact).

3.3.4.1

As your downswing starts and proceeds forward, gravity will be pulling your body backward. The weight on your back foot will be intense, and your balance will feel really bad. If you can learn to deal with it, however, you can hit really good uphill shots. They will launch higher, carry shorter and stop quicker, so use more club (less loft). And after impact, when the ball is gone, it's OK to fall back.

3.3.4.2

3.4 Controlling Launch Direction and In-flight Curvature

"I can't hit the ball straight … so why should I learn to hit it crooked"? I've heard this question many, many times; and I have the answer (two reasons) for it:

1) Learn to hit it crooked so you can get out of the trouble you will get into
2) Learning to hit it crooked will teach you something about not hitting it crooked (which helps you hit it straighter)

You need to curve shots to successfully play with Damage Control. No doubt; no question; no choice; you need to be able to curve shots to avoid disaster holes. Plus the added benefit of learning how to curve shots also makes it easier to learn how not to curve them!

The launch direction, elevation and spin of your shots are always affected by the angle of your clubface, relative to your swing path direction through impact. Learning how to hit shots with your clubface accurately opened or closed makes it easier to curve shots around obstacles and escape from trouble like the pros.

3.4.1 The clubface affects launch direction and spin

Four facets of reality all golfers must deal with are:

> 1) The launch direction of a shot is affected seriously by the clubface angle (aim) and to a lesser extent by its travel direction (path) through impact
> 2) Clubface aim at impact can be controlled by changing either your clubface aim or your grip at address
> 3) Clubface rotation can be maximized or minimized by promoting or inhibiting your forearm release through impact
> 4) In-flight curvature is determined by clubface angle relative to swing path direction through impact

The simplest way to curve shots (fades and slices or draws and hooks) for most golfers is to set the clubface at address in exactly the impact position desired for the shot, then grip it normally and swing away. The shot will launch in a direction determined primarily by the clubface angle at impact. The ball will then spin and curve away from that direction, based on the severity of the glancing blow caused by the clubface angle relative to the swing path direction (Figure 3.4.1.1).

3.4.1.1

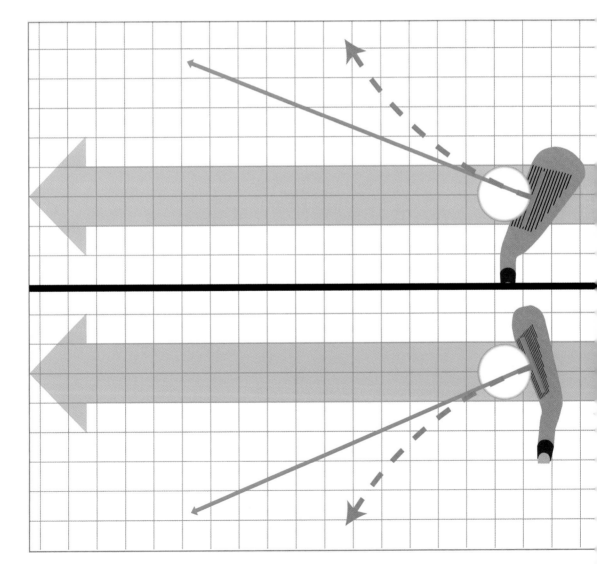

There is another option, however, and many Tour professionals accomplish curving shots in the opposite way. They leave their clubface square at address but pre-set their grip to a different position, so their clubface turns to the angle they want through impact as their hands return to their normal (square) impact position. They've practiced their swings with square clubface alignment so often their hand positions are grooved to return to square through impact. This repeatability allows them to preset their hands (grips) to different positions at address (Figure 3.4.1.2), knowing their hands will return to square and create the cut or draw face angles they desire at impact.

3.4.1.2

Normal   Cut   Draw

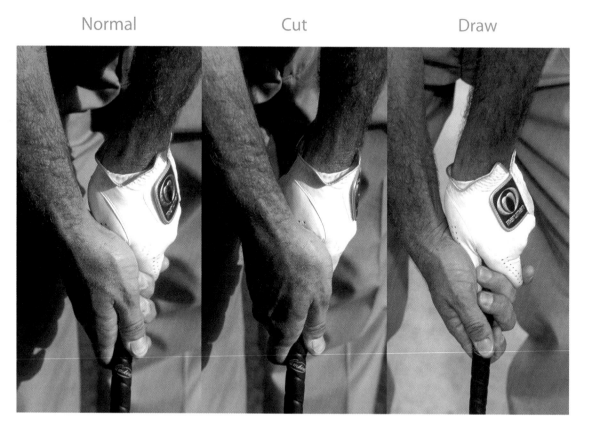

3.4.2 Open clubfaces creates slices

Let's say you've hit your ball behind a big tree, and the best way to get back into the game is to play around the left side of it. The easiest way to produce a slice every time is by simply aiming left and hitting the ball with an open clubface. The problem with this shot (a slice) is many golfers don't allow enough room for the ball to start to the right of their swing line (they expect the shot to fly straight first, then slice).

A serious slice can be seen in Figure 3.4.2.1 on the next page. Notice how I aim way left of the big tree, to assure my ball doesn't hit the tree straight-away off my clubface. This "start-to-the-right" then "slice-more-to-the-right" shot is invaluable to a good Damage Control game, and it's simple to hit. But you must learn how far right the ball will start, and then how much it will slice, before you can aim your set-up and swing, and play it with confidence. I'll show you the drill to learn both later in Chapter 7.

3.4.3 Closed clubfaces create hooks

Hooks can be created in the opposite way (from slices), with a glancing blow from a closed face through impact. The closed face will start the ball left, and then the spin will make it hook farther to the left from there. The same precautions apply to this shot also, except in the opposite direction. Most golfers don't allow enough room for the left start off the clubface, and too often hit straight into the trouble they are trying to avoid.

A serious hook shot can be seen in Figure 3.4.3.1. See how far to the right I am set-up, to allow for the initial launch to the left? This start-left-then-hook shot is also valuable to Damage Control. Again, you must learn how far left the ball will start, and how far it will hook, before you can use it on course. A drill for this learning will also be demonstrated in Chapter 7.

3.4.2.1

3.4.3.1

It is important to note: there is another way to affect the curvature of shots using your hands and forearms; either by rotating (flipping over) the clubface extremely rapidly, or turning it in the opposite direction (blocking) from normal through impact. It's counter productive to this book, however, to teach these moves here. Remember, in Damage Control we are interested only in one thing … getting out of trouble in one shot … so you can control the damage to your score once you find yourself in trouble. We want to do this in the simplest way possible. Even Tour pros get into deep trouble trying to hit fancy shots around obstacles from trouble lies.

It's never wise to exacerbate your swing problems when in trouble. Always use the simplest technique available to get out of trouble, and back into the game. Don't let your ego slip into the equation of trying overly difficult shots from bad lies.

3.5 The Good and Bad News of Swing Shaping

Being able to change the shape of your swing is critical. In a reasonably sized book we could never detail all the swing shapes necessary to play from the almost infinite number of trouble shots you will encounter in your golfing future. But it isn't necessary anyway, because memorizing particular swings isn't what Damage Control is about. The skill you need is to be able to understand what kind of swing shape each new trouble situation demands in your mind's eye, and then be able to create such a swing physically within reasonable tolerances.

The key to success in doing this lies in understanding why and how to make swing changes. Once you comprehend what set-up postures affect which body parts to deliver the particular swings you need, actually making them becomes pretty easy. Golfers who have never experienced swinging and hitting shots in different and creative ways, can really have fun learning this skill of Damage Control. It's important to understand; creating different and effective swings is not difficult, it's just different.

First let me give you the bad news: to better escape from trouble, changing the shape of your swing requires several things different from what you've practiced before, so many they would be difficult to memorize.

By:

- Gripping down on the shaft
- Leaning forward
- Changing the timing of your hand / wrist action

You can change how much room your swing requires behind the ball.

By:

- Positioning your spine-angle properly
- Rotating the appropriate part of your body (upper / lower)
- Keeping your arms connected to your chest

You can execute powerful swings in very flat or upright planes.

By:

- Leaning so your spine is perpendicular to the ground
- Emphasizing your upper body and arm swing
- Learning to swing in balance, when balance is different than normal and difficult to maintain

You can conquer the problems sloping terrains present.

By:

- Controlling setting-up with your clubface properly aimed at address
- Creating that face angle accurately through impact

You can affect the starting direction and curvature of your ball, to avoid hitting trouble in your immediate vicinity.

But now, the good news: you don't have to remember them. In fact, once you understand and feel the fundamentals of changing the shape of your swing, it's virtually impossible to forget them. With a little practice (in your backyard, Chapter 7), it is absolutely reasonable for golfers of all skill levels to remember the feel of executing swings of different shapes, and hitting trouble shots reasonably solidly (producing reasonable results).

Even better news is you don't have to be an expert swing shaper … to play with Damage Control. You simply have to be adequate at it. The requirement of swing shaping is only to hit a good enough shot to get the ball back somewhere into the game on your first attempt. The shot doesn't have to be perfect. It just has to end up somewhere decent, in a safe lie. Then you can make a good shot to recover and possibly avoid losing a stroke.

If only the rest of the game, your normal game, was this easy!

For most normal golf shots the less tightness, tension, grip pressure and activity in your hands through impact, the better. In fact for the short game and putting I recommend only enough grip pressure to keep the club from coming loose and flying away during the swing. This "hold-on-only" function for your hands does not always work, however, when hitting escape shots from trouble.

Think about a ball in a patch of knee-high grass lying down in an inch of water. Imagine the feel in your hands, wrists and forearms as you force your swing down and through the grass and water to contact the ball. Focus on the intensity of effort you would apply through impact to blast the ball up and out of this mess. This total effort, this fire in your hands, is the "hand-fire" of Damage Control.

Feeling the correct hand-fire for trouble shots is the third skill of Damage Control. While it's probably more difficult to define than it is to learn, you shouldn't play without hand-fire feel. Because when normal swings won't work from trouble, knowing how to turn up your hand-fire may be your only way out!

4.1 Hand-Fire is a Feel

The effort you expend in your grip pressure, your hand action and the brute force you apply through impact, all combine to form your hand-fire for a given swing from trouble (Figure 4.0.1). The energy you supply through each of these components of hand-fire contributes to the motion, speed and power of your golf swing. The intensity of effort in these components creates the total hand-fire you supply to a shot, and controls the speed and momentum your clubhead possesses at it moves through impact with the golf ball. Hand-fire is energy, effort, the application of pressure and force.

The feel of hand-fire deals with feeling how much effort should be applied through the hands, wrists, and forearms to power golf swings through impact, when some resistance to such force exists. Notice I said through impact, not to it. I know you can't physically feel the various degrees of hand-fire sitting in a chair reading this book. But if you examine enough examples (as you'll see below) in your mind's eye, however, you can begin to understand hand-fire intellectually.

Then when you get out on a course you will reap a benefit. As you create different swings for different trouble shots, by focusing on the feel in your hands through impact you will internalize your own scale (feel) of hand-fire. That's the goal of this chapter: to get you to first recognize, then feel, the hand-fire needed to execute successful escape shots from trouble.

4.0.1 - The Hand-Fire Equation

$$HF = GP + HA + BF$$

Hand Fire   Grip Pressure   Hand Action   Brute Force

4.1.1 Grip pressure (GP)

Grip pressure resides mainly in the fingers with a little involvement into the palms of the hands. It can be rated on a scale from zero to ten (zero would not be holding a club, 10 would be squeezing it as hard as you possibly can). For normal golf shots, grip pressure increases with increasing clubhead speed to counter greater outward forces generated by higher swing speeds. Golfers instinctively increase their grip pressure as they swing faster, to keep the club from flying out of their hands and down the fairway.

Rating grip pressure for normal shots, I estimate the value for normal putts at 2, and for half-wedge finesse shots (from around 40-yards) from good lies on level terrain at 3. As grip pressure decreases to lower values (below 3), the pressure and tension in your hands decreases, giving you better sensitivity for delicate touch and feel, but less capability of power. At a grip pressure of 2 if you were to make a full wedge swing, the club would slip, and at a pressure of 1 it would fly out of your hands shortly after impact.

You can "see" grip pressure if you get close enough to watch some of the world's best player's hands. In Figure 4.1.1.1, the late Payne Stewart is chipping from the fringe to a fast green, as so often encountered on the PGA Tour. I would guess his grip pressure for this shot would be no more than 2, and for sure less than for his normal half-wedge shot.

4.1.1.1 - Payne Stewart/GP = 2

4.1.1.2 - Fred Couples/GP=2

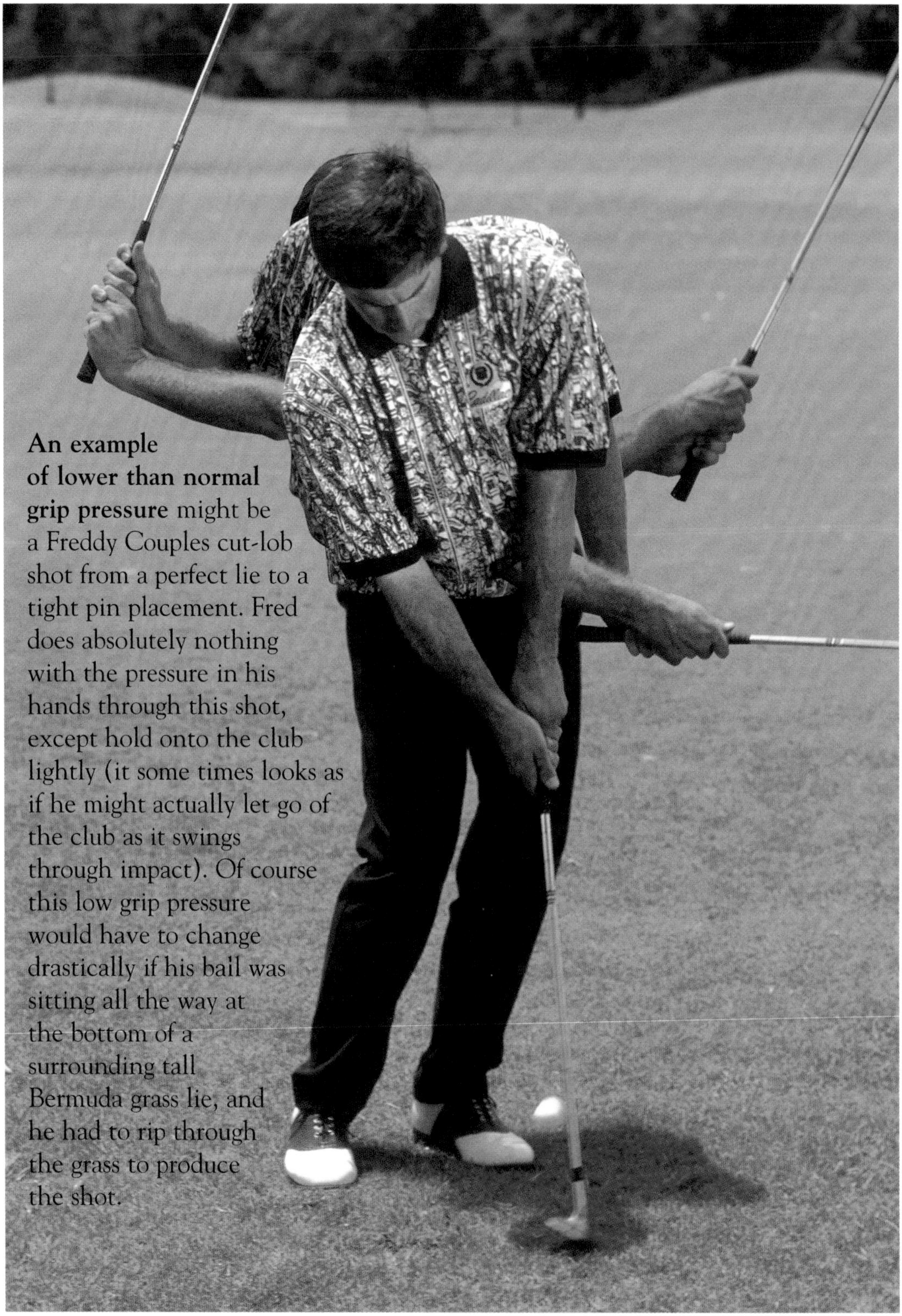

An example of lower than normal grip pressure might be a Freddy Couples cut-lob shot from a perfect lie to a tight pin placement. Fred does absolutely nothing with the pressure in his hands through this shot, except hold onto the club lightly (it some times looks as if he might actually let go of the club as it swings through impact). Of course this low grip pressure would have to change drastically if his ball was sitting all the way at the bottom of a surrounding tall Bermuda grass lie, and he had to rip through the grass to produce the shot.

Moving to a normal wedge swing, look at Lee Janzen's 40-yard wedge shot from a good lie in light rough (Figure 4.1.1.3). Lee uses very quiet hands (which is a good thing when precision is required) and would qualify for no higher than a 3 grip pressure. I would also estimate a pressure of 4 for the distance wedge swing of Steve Elkington, in Figure 4.1.1.4. Because Elk's shot carry distance is longer than Janzen's shot, I'm sure he held onto the club with a little more pressure in his fingers and hands. As you can see however, he is not squeezing the club and he doesn't have a death-grip on it. He doesn't exert any excess pressure, which helps him achieve his excellent distance control and touch in these shots.

4.1.1.3 - Lee Janzen/GP=3

4.1.1.4 - Steve Elkington/GP=4

Increasing outward forces are generated through higher swing speeds on longer shots. Correspondingly, the grip pressure necessary to hold onto clubs naturally increases also, but shouldn't normally get too high. You can see good grips in the 7-iron swing of Phil Mickelson (Figure 4.1.1.5) and the drive of Vijay Singh (Figure 4.1.1.6). Vijay has his right hand grip almost off the club through impact and it's clear he's only holding-on with his left. The good news here is Vijay exerts no manipulation of his driver face through impact, swinging with a motion powered purely by his body and arm rotation. His hold-on-only grip pressure through this shot may be no more than 6, even though he is one of the longest drivers on Tour.

4.1.1.5 - Phil Mickelson/GP=5

4.1.1.6 - Vijay Singh/GP=6

You can imagine for all the above shots, if there was trouble (behind, in front of, over, or under the ball) which needed to be moved as the ball was hit, the player's grip pressure would need to increase in every case. This increase would constitute a part of their hand-fire for the shot.

One last thought about grip pressure: If you use a super-tight "death" grip and excessive wrist tension in your normal game for normal shots, it will cause touch and feel problems. I'm not talking about that. I'm discussing increased grip pressure (and other increased hand-fire contributions below) only in the light of Damage Control shots from trouble. If you have a problem with excessive grip pressure in your normal game, take care of it as part of a normal game improvement program with your local golf professional.

4.1.2 Hand Action (HA)

A golfer's hand action is the combination of his wrist motion (cocking, un-cocking, or hinging), forearm rotation and hand-controlled club manipulations. Some amount of hand action occurs in normal golf shots (except putts). Refer to Figure 4.1.2.1 A-C to see: A) wrist hinge (not used in a normal swing), B) wrist cock, and C) forearm rotation.

The hand action we are concerned with in Damage Control is the non-normal hand action above or below that which occurs in normal shots with good lies from the same distance. We generally refer to hand action on its own scale from zero to ten, with zero indicating no hand action what-so-ever, and 10 the maximum amount possible.

Damage Control often requires hand action to deliver extra effort and control when attempting to curve shots in non-normal trajectories. This includes control of the clubhead path and face to be unique and different in some way from normal.

4.1.2.1 A - Wrist hinge

4.1.2.1 B – Wrist cock

4.1.2.1 C – Forearm rotation

Hand action is not instinctive, and in many instances is never even considered by golfers. As you'll see in photographs to follow, when increased hand-fire is demanded from trouble, a player had better know both how and how much to apply, or be doomed to failure.

The point of even talking about hand action is that so many golfers don't ever change their wrist cock or forearm rotation to benefit their shots. They either don't think about it, or they don't know how to do it. Their hand action always stays the same even when they try to extricate balls from deep trouble. And this "just doesn't cut it" for the purposes of Damage Control.

The more delicate the shot, the lower the hand action. As finesse shots around the green become more delicate, and a softer, more finely tuned touch is required, less than normal hand action is required. In fact, for some shots, removing all hand-action can be beneficial to shot results.

To see some examples of hand action, let's again look at some shots. As we see the great Gary Player chipping with a bladed wedge in Figure 4.1.2.2, his grip is very light and he does nothing more than hold onto the club with his hands. A Fred Couples pitch and ball toss to a fast green (Figure 4.1.2.3) also looks soft and gentle; I don't see Freddie adding any effort to his normal soft hand action for this shot, and I can't imagine anyone doing it better.

4.1.2.2 - Gary Player/HA=2

4.1.2.3 - Fred Couples/HA=2

Here I'm making my dead-hands-dead-wrist chip as if to a super-fast green running downhill away from me (Figure 4.1.2.4). This is a zero hand action shot. I use no wrist cock, no forearm rotation, and am barely holding on to the club to caress this shot as softly onto the green as I possibly can!

4.1.2.4 - HA=0

The control of hand action for club manipulation requires more (moderate) effort. As a need for manipulation of your clubhead arises in trouble shots, a need for hand action to control them also becomes a requirement. This point is paramount to your understanding of hand-fire. When you take a normal swing through impact, you get a normal shot reaction. If a normal shot reaction is not what you want, however, something has to change the way your club passes through impact to make the ball do something different. That something is hand action.

In Figure 4.1.2.5, I'm hitting a knock-down 9-iron shot between two trees on the 14th hole at Pinehurst #2. Because I want the shot to stay low but also have lots of backspin, I'm keeping my hands ahead of the club through impact. I'm delaying the normal release of my forearms and hooding the clubface to keep the ball from flying to the right. I feel this modest amount of extra hand action (compared to normal) requires a rating of 5.

4.1.2.5 - HA=5

Now look at the hands of one of the best-ever finesse players, Ben Crenshaw, as he draws a shot around trees with a punch-shot swing (Figure 4.1.2.6) with hand action of 6. Please note; if you think I don't have the correct values of hand action for this swing, that's fine, use your own. The important point to understand is, the more pressure and force you transfer from your hands, wrists and forearms to the ball through impact (to control the shot's flight trajectory), the greater your hand action must be.

4.1.2.6 Bene Crenshaw (Draw)/HA = 6

Severiano Ballesterous (Seve) has tremendous hand action through some of his shots. Some of his escapes are legendary inside the professional player ranks, leading to descriptions of "unbelievable," "absurd" and "impossible!" A rather mundane shot for him is shown in Figure 4.1.2.7, using a hand action of 6 to control the hook of this shot around the tree blocking his vision of the hole (it's not easy to make a wedge shot hook).

4.1.2.7 - Seve/HA=6

Instead of rolling their hands over through impact to produce a dramatic hook, sometimes a player needs to use hand-fire to control a club to do exactly the opposite. By this I mean manipulation of the club to not turn over, to hold the clubface open as it passes past impact, to block the normal rotation of clubface closure through impact. Unquestionably, one of the most creative and talented professionals to ever play the game, in terms of trouble shots in general and the "hold-clubface-open-for-super-high-shots" in particular, is Phil Mickelson (Figure 4.1.2.8). In both of these shots, Phil uses a hand action of 7 to hold the clubface open well past impact, until after he has launched his shot.

4.1.2.8 - Phil Mickelson/HA=7

An example of even stronger hand action is the action sequence of Gary Player shown in Figure 4.1.2.9. Notice his wrists immediately after impact. Even though his hands have not continued to move through and past their impact position (as they would in a normal swing motion), he has completed his post impact wrist re-cock action. This hand action requires both strength and tremendous timing to produce effective shot results, and warrants a hand action rating of 9.

4.1.2.9 - Gary Player/HA=9

4.1.3 Brute Force

As a man who specializes in teaching the short game, finesse shots and putting, I almost cringe when it comes time to talk about using brute force in the golf swing. When our research shows it is necessary, however, I've got to do it.

Brute force is the extra effort and power a golfer must provide (from the body, hands and arms) to create stability and power his club through the extraordinary resistance sometimes encountered in a golf shot. In addition to strong grip pressure and active hands, brute force is quite often required to power a club through water, grass, bushes, or whatever surrounds a ball in seriously troubled lies. While you may not have thought about it, I'm sure you've experienced it.

In normal sand shots, because you need to move some sand forward in addition to the ball, you use enough hand-fire to provide extra speed for your club head into and through impact. This shot does not, however, require any significant brute force. Brute force is required when you need to cut through long grass behind the ball, so your club can get to the ball with significant clubhead speed. It is then needed to continue moving the club through impact and all resistance past impact, to make sure the ball gets out of the trouble.

This same brute force can be necessary to move water, sand, weeds, mud … whatever your ball is in. The body plays a large part in supplying brute force, by providing a stable foundation from which to launch these extra-powerful swings, a base to push both with and against.

Let me show you an example of a shot where brute force is required. When a ball comes in high and hard, landing in heavy sand, you can get a lie as shown in Figure 4.1.3.1. To get this ball up and onto the green, a clubface angle which will dig deeply enough to get below the ball (Figure 4.1.3.2) is required. Then all the sand around the ball, along with the ball itself, must be moved out of the bunker.

4.1.3.1

4.1.3.2

4.1.3.3

The problem is, when the leading edge of the club digs into the sand, the club won't bounce off the sand to keep the sand divot shallow and maintain its speed through the impact zone. This means the club must be powered by brute force, especially after initial impact with the sand (Figure 4.1.3.3), to move all this weight forward.

Look at what happens to this same shot if I make a normal swing effort with no hand-fire. What a disaster!

4.1.3.4

Now that you understand there can be a brute force component to hand-fire, be sure to notice when it plays a part in the overall hand-fire requirements of upcoming examples.

4.1.4 Hand-fire (HF) intensity

The three factors that make up the Hand Fire equation (Grip Pressure plus Hand Action plus Brute Force) combine to give each trouble shot an overall "Hand-fire" value. We (at the Pelz Golf Institute) often refer to hand fire on a scale from zero to ten, ten representing the maximum possible amount of hand-fire you can deliver. Of course this is an arbitrary scale, based on the research, teaching and coaching we've done over the years.

If a shot requires only a little extra grip pressure to keep the club stable through some light rough, then the hand-fire needed is low. When some faster than normal wrist action and forearm rotation is added to an increased grip pressure, the hand-fire rating goes up. And when brute force must be added to the mix through impact, the hand-fire goes up again. What about when you need to bludgeon a club through tall, thick, wet grass, and the ball is sitting down in water? In some cases the requirement for hand-fire can run all the way up to ten, and you might be well advised to take a drop with a one-stroke penalty when it does!

To get a sense of what hand-fire feels like, I suggest you pick up a short iron club and feel the hand-fire manipulations shown on the following two pages (Figures 4.1.4.1ab and 4.1.4.2ab).

4.1.4.1A

Here you see **normal** backswing wrist cock timing.

4.1.4.1B

Now you see a stepped-up (**quicker**) wrist cock in the backswing. The faster you complete your wrist cock in the backswing, the later you will un-cock your wrists on the down swing, and the earlier you'll cock them on the through swing (after impact). The more quickly you execute your wrist cock motions, the higher the hand-fire rating of your swing.

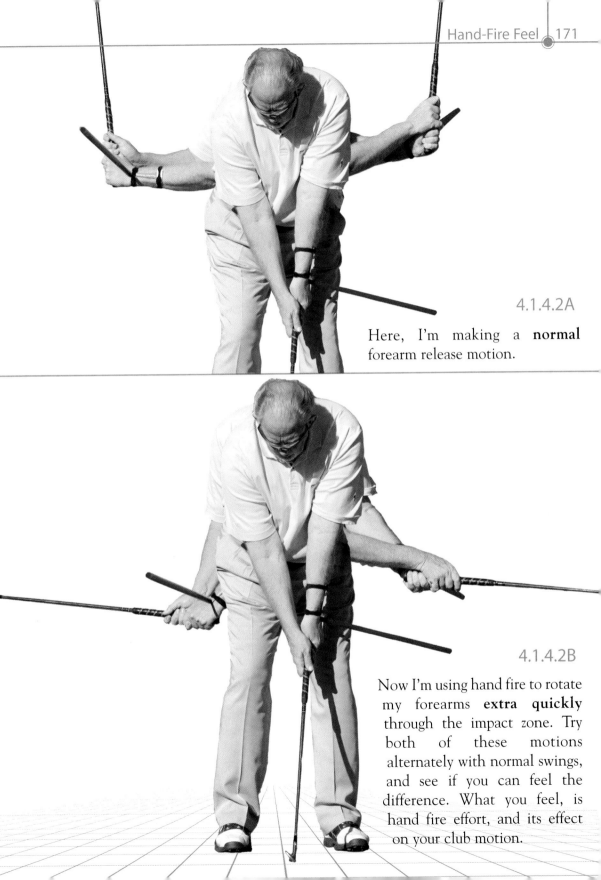

4.1.4.2A

Here, I'm making a **normal** forearm release motion.

4.1.4.2B

Now I'm using hand fire to rotate my forearms **extra quickly** through the impact zone. Try both of these motions alternately with normal swings, and see if you can feel the difference. What you feel, is hand fire effort, and its effect on your club motion.

In Figure 4.1.4.3 I'm making a block-cut manipulation through impact with a 1-pound weight on my club head. Try this to feel the hand fire of a cut-shot block swing. This is the move you will need to curve a shot to the right, by making sure the club face is open through impact (relative to the club head path).

4.1.4.3

The **hand-fire used to manipulate a clubface** is usually less than the effort required to cut through stuff around the golf ball, especially when your ball lies in serious trouble. I feel like I simulate a feel of higher hand-fire when I shove a box full of books across the carpet. This starts to involve a brute force component in the hand-fire, and creates much more pressure up the back of my left hand, in both wrist joints, and in my arms up to my shoulders (Figure 4.1.4.4).

4.1.4.4

Interested in the feel of the ultimate hand-fire including lots of brute force? Try pushing your club against something really solid from your impact position (Figure 4.1.4.5). Don't swing into this, just lay your club on it, and then push to feel the force. This might be similar to what it feels like to cut through 8-inch high, wet, U.S. Open rough, trying to get all the way down to a ball sitting on the ground. You never honestly know if you can get your club through it or not!

4.1.4.5

4.2 From a Little Smoke, to Smoldering, to Imminent Fire

If you're not feeling what hand-fire is yet, don't worry. When you see enough real swings involving higher values of hand-fire (coming later in this book), then go to a golf course and make these swings yourself, you'll know immediately what we mean.

Even though most golfers never practice shots from buried-in-sand lies, or from deep rough, or out of water, you ... a golfer who wants to play with Damage Control ... should do just that. And you can to do it in your backyard! After you get through doing the drills of Damage Control as recommended in Chapter 7, the feel of hand-fire will be surging through your veins.

4.2.1 A little smoke

Good lies in light rough don't require much (if any) hand-fire at all, and curving shots with hand-fire require only a small increase in hand action and club manipulation effort. When balls sit down in grass more than 4-inches high, however, the need for serious hand-fire (a little smoke) becomes a reality.

Almost any ball in 4-inch or longer bluegrass or Bermuda grass rough, especially if wet, will require serious hand-fire smoke to produce consistent shot results. Similarly, if one were to find their ball in a fried-egg lie in sand, or in casual water (the bottom of the ball sitting in water, with no good drop area available), these conditions also provide resistance to the clubhead through impact, and bring the requirement of a little smoke.

The 1999 U.S. Open at Pinehurst #2 had what I believe is the perfect length Bermuda grass rough. At 4 to 4 and 1/2-inches, most Bermuda grass roughs (Figure 4.2.1.1) will let a golf ball sink to its bottom, while still giving the golfer a good view of the ball. This leads golfers (after driving into the rough) to believe they can get a good strike on the ball and get it to the green. The difficulty of this shot entails not only having enough hand-fire to extricate the ball with enough power to reach the green, but then stopping it once it gets there (shots have minimal backspin from this lie).

4.2.1.1

Similarly for balls sitting slightly down in raked furrows (or un-raked foot prints) in the sand, hand-fire of at least 5 is required. This "smoke" is needed to carry the club head into, through and out of the sand with enough speed to carry a ball 10-yards up onto the green (Figure 4.2.1.2). Again the problem of not enough backspin often causes this shot to be doubly difficult to stop close to the pin.

4.2.1.2

4.2.2 Smoldering hands

Even stronger hand-fire is necessary to extract balls from worse rough grass conditions and when they are more deeply imbedded into sand. When a ball finds 6 to 8-inch high rough grass, the chance of not being able to get the ball out on the first swing starts to become a reality. The same applies when balls plug into sand and more than half the ball remains below the surface. The reason for a hand-fire requirement in these cases is obvious; a brute force component of hand-fire is needed to power the clubhead through the grass and/or sand, and continue the motion of the club far enough past impact to assure the ball moves safely forward and out of the trouble.

Look at the greenside swing of Vijay Singh (Figure 4.2.2.1) with a ball sitting down in tough Bermuda grass, just 5 steps off the practice green at the Eastlake Golf Club in Atlanta, home of the PGA Tour Championship. Notice his hand action intensity and the motion of the clubhead immediately after impact. Now imagine how this shot might turn out if he had used only the normal light grip pressure required to carry a shot 7-yards from a perfect lie. His club would have probably stopped cold when it encountered the "sticky-resistance" from this grass. I think you can see, and perhaps imagine a little, the feel of hand-fire used in Damage Control.

4.2.2.1

4.2.3.1

4.2.3 Imminent fire

When a hand-fire of 7 or 8 is required to extricate a ball from trouble, you know you are in a potentially serious, as in disaster score serious, situation. Several examples of this are similar to lies in the previous section (4.2.2), but now the ball is buried completely below the surface of wet, heavy sand (Figure 4.2.3.1 previous page). In these cases the sand has absorbed moisture and isheavier, stronger, and more densely packed. This increases the mass and resistance, and makes it even more difficult (requiring more club speed, momentum and brute force) to move a clubhead and ball through.

Notice the effort Tom Sieckmann, Director of Instruction in our Scoring Game Schools, has put into his "toe-in-first" escape from a completely buried lie in Figure 4.2.3.2.

4.2.3.2

4.3 Open Flames to Full Blast Furnace

Maximum hand-fire from a strong player can blast through a surprising amount of long wet grass, sand, dirt, sticks, bushes, branches, water and anything else in the way of a successful escape shot. Of course, such effort and energy are not advisable for use in golf and the concept of avoidance usually produces far superior results. There are times, however, when maximum grip pressure, hand action and brute force...maximum hand-fire...must be applied.

4.3.1 Open flames

A need for open flame hand-fire occurs after you've driven a ball into the lip of a fairway sand bunker and it plugs all the way under the sand on a severe up-slope. Moving this much sand will take a hand-fire effort of 8 to get the ball cleanly out (Figure 4.3.1.1). (Note: In this shot the up-slope was so steep I couldn't lean back far enough to eliminate a bad spine angle with the sand, and still keep my balance. This wasn't a problem, however, because the sand didn't hurt my hands or wrists when my club stopped directly in the sand after impact.)

4.3.1.1- HF=8

Another example of open flames hand-fire intensity can be seen in the image of Thongchai Jaidee from a fairway bunker at the 2004 PGA Championship at Whistling Straits (Figure 4.3.1.2). As can be imagined from this photograph, without strong hand action through impact, this ball would never have gotten up and out of the sand.

4.3.1.2- HF=8

There are zillions of water hazards around the world, many of which have transition edges that trap golf balls, tempting dangerous escape shot attempts. Partially submerged balls in water and muck present an interesting dichotomy to golfers. This shot encourages one to lay the clubface partially open so the bottom of the club will splash and bounce off the water, not letting the club dig in too deeply while keeping the club head speed up. Yet, the clubface needs to be closed enough to allow deep enough penetration to achieve club face contact with the ball. Solid club to ball contact is necessary to power the ball up and out of the goop (Figure 4.3.1.3). Once these clubface angle requirements are correctly balanced for a shot, a hand-fire effort of at least 8 must be applied through impact to finish-off the escape!

4.3.2 Blast furnace hand-fire

The reason for showing this much hand-fire is not to encourage you to use it. Rather, it's my belief that seeing photographs of players successfully getting out of the worst kind of fire trouble can be influential in helping you get your arms around the concept of hand-fire. I believe understanding always helps the learning and internalization process. I also believe it's good to know what zero and maximum (10) hand-fire feels like in order to refine your feel and use it in appropriate levels for Damage Control in your own game.

When a ball is completely submerged in water it can be successfully blasted out with a square club face. This face angle allows the club to dig into the water, if you have enough hand-fire power to make it do so. Success for this shot depends upon a player's ability to create a very high swing speed before entering the water, then apply enough hand-fire (which takes plentiful wrist and forearm strength) to maintain clubhead velocity through and after impact. Just such power is demonstrated in the full-out blast by Masters Champion Craig Stadler (Figure 4.3.2.1).

4.3.2.1- Craig Stadler/HF=10

Similar swing speeds and hand-fire strength are needed to bludgeon balls out of the foot-high wet bluegrass roughs, weeds, and liquid fertilized grasses used in surrounding fairways in important tournaments today. When the pros encounter such trouble, they use their well-conditioned wrists and forearms to apply the maximum hand-fire to blast their balls back into the game (Figure 4.3.2.2).

4.3.2.2- Tiger Woods/HF=Max

4.4 Hand-Fire Feel is Essential in Damage Control

The lessons of this chapter for learning the skill of hand-fire feel are simple. Grip pressure is a component of hand-fire and must be changed from trouble shot to trouble shot. The speeds or quickness with which you cock, un-cock, and re-cock your wrists, rotate your forearms, and manipulate your hands through your swing are also components of hand-fire. Additionally there is the application of brute force to bludgeon your way through stuff around your balls in seriously troubled lies.

While it is natural to hold onto your clubs with normal grip pressure and use some hand action in normal golf shots, the correct adjustment and application of hand-fire is a skill of Damage Control to be learned. It is fundamental to success in escaping from trouble situations.

To play with Damage Control one must apply hand-fire to control and manipulate your club to curve balls around, or extricate them from, whatever trouble you find on the course. Don't think the application of hand-fire runs counter to the teaching of normal swings. I want to assure you: We're not trying to change that teaching … we're adding to it!

You need to know; you can't hit a ball out of water with a normal swing using normal effort and grip pressure. And you can't get a ball out of tall grass or deep sand with a nice smooth finesse swing. And you can't adjust your shot trajectories away from normal without applying hand-fire somewhere in your swing.

Hand-fire feel is the third skill of Damage Control. It's a skill you need to be aware of, and become moderately proficient at using, if you're going to save yourself in the future … from your disaster holes and scores of yester-year!

Beautiful swing, nice shot ... but, ... but, ... but, ... ohhhhhhh, ... too bad!

There is nothing more discouraging than seeing your perfectly-struck escape shot land just like you wanted it to in the center of the green, only to watch it bounce over the back, down the hill and into the water. This is especially agonizing when it leads you into a disasterous score and ruins your round.

The fourth skill of Damage Control is Red Flag Touch. It involves a little red flag attached to your temple, connected directly through into your brain. When you're preparing to play from trouble and your red flag pops up, it issues a brain alert.

Look-out ... you're in danger! If you don't play this shot carefully, it won't stop until it finds more trouble. You are in red-flag danger; be alert and focused; plan and play carefully. Do NOT hit this shot from the frying pan ... into the fire!

Having red flag touch is having the skill to: 1) listen to red flag warnings, 2) understand what they mean, and 3) play extra-carefully with enough touch to insure trouble shots to red flag areas end up safely.

5.1 The Meaning of Red-Flag Touch

Red-flag touch is entirely different from the first three skills of Damage Control (set-up-ology, swing shaping, and hand-fire feel) detailed in previous chapters. Those skills involve setting-up properly for trouble shots, shaping swings to work from trouble lies, and feeling how to transfer effort, control and power through your hands into escape shots. They all three deal with how and what you do before and during the execution of escape swings from trouble.

Red-flag touch involves understanding and planning for what's going to happen after you launch escape shots: how far they will fly, where they'll land, how they might bounce, and most importantly, where they'll stop. The acquisition of red-flag touch and its internalization into your game will involve combining acute observational awareness with trouble shot experience. The result will enable you to visualize … even predict … how trouble shots will react to the red-flag conditions into which you play them.

5.1.1 Red-flag status

Red-flag status initiates when you find yourself in an incredibly bad lie, you can't predict your shot pattern, and you're in the vicinity of severe fire trouble (Figure 5.1.1.1). Firmness or softness of landing areas, a sloped landing surface, surface contours, hazards, obstacles, or the speed of green surfaces themselves can cause your shots to end up in serious trouble and trigger that red flag to pop up in your brain.

When your escape shots face conditions such that a reasonably well-executed swing will launch a ball which may still end up in another frying-pan or even a fire lie, a red-flag should go up in your brain. And when the red-flag goes up … you should get goose-pimples on your skin. The goose-pimples mean you are alert … ready … you are aware and focused. You'll play this shot with an extra amount of care and attention, and with a conservative enough approach … to avoid a disastrous result.

5.1.1.1

5.1.2 Red-flag trajectories

The trajectories of shots from trouble are more difficult to control, and miss their desired flight path more frequently and by greater amounts, than do normal shots. Probably more than one-half of all trouble shots come out higher and softer, with significantly less energy than planned. The rest (very few come out perfectly) come out hotter, with lower trajectories than expected. Both results cause serious problems because in trouble scenarios you never know which one is coming next.

There are times, for whatever reason, as you stand over a ball in trouble, you feel you might skull your escape shot. At other times you might fear hitting it fat. In either of these situations your red-flag should pop up and send the alert: back-off, reconsider the swing you are about to make.

There may be something wrong with your set-up and you need to do something to better control how high or how hard this shot will fly out from this mess. Or you may need to re-verify your ball position or reconsider your target selection. Remember, the red flag is telling you: "There's something wrong, so be careful. We can't afford a really bad performance now … we are in red-flag territory here!"

5.1.3 Red-flag backspin

The more debris that comes between your ball and the clubface through impact, the less backspin your shot will have. The more obstacles bothering your swing, making you change its shape to avoid collision with the club, the less solidly you're likely to hit the shot. For both these reasons, escape shots quite often don't have good backspin.

This causes the result of not knowing quite what to expect when the lie is somewhere between clean and nesty. Will your trouble shot come out at the bottom end of the backspin spectrum, with essentially zero spin (Figure 5.1.3.1 red)? Or will it come out almost normally, with normal backspin (white)? From all such lies, your red-flag warning should be audible. Be careful, this ball may run forever after it lands or at least until it runs into some kind of trouble.

5.2 Red-Flags for Surface Conditions

Golf is played on many surfaces, and the condition of most of them vary with weather and time. Grass on greens grows, gets mowed and rolled. Thatch below the grass surface is compacted and aerated. Fairway and rough grasses grow and get cut, moisture absorbs and evaporates, sand compacts and gets raked, tree limbs extend and get trimmed, and water levels rise and fall. Around the world, even on any given course, the conditions under which we play the game are virtually never the same.

As surface conditions change, most are reasonably benign to the play of golfers and are considered "part of the game" for the day. There are a few surface conditions, however, which can cause significant changes in ball reactions, precipitate disaster holes, and ruin scores. These are classified as red-flag surface conditions.

5.2.1 Super-soft

Have you ever lost a ball in the middle of the fairway? Probably not, unless it flew into a low lying, wet, super-soft area and plugged deep into the ground. Because this is seldom the case, we don't worry much about it. I want to assure you, however, it happens (I have lost several balls in such conditions because I enjoy playing even in the rain and cold).

When you do play into such an area, after 100-year rains have deluged it, a red-flag alert should pop-up to remind you: keep all shots into this area on low flight trajectories. This will keep the shots landing at low attack angles and hopefully keep them from plugging into the surface and disappearing from sight.

5.2.2 Firm and hard

Hard approaches and hard greens also signal red-flag alerts. When green complexes contain trouble and green surfaces are so firm that all pitch marks disappear, a red-flag should pop up. When approaches and greens are so hard balls bounce three feet or more into the air, red-flags should also go up. These conditions make all chipping, pitching and wedge shots more difficult to play, even for well struck shots from good lies. Their inhospitable attitude toward trouble shots with no backspin leads directly to disaster and is good reason for issuing red-flag alerts on their behalf.

When fairways become hard like airport runways, it can be very difficult to stop drives within their boundaries. Firm fairway surfaces let balls run-on, stopping only when they get into the higher grasses of the rough. When this happens, the course is said to be playing hard and fast and, if roughs are also long and penal, scoring over the entire round will run higher than normal. These conditions don't elicit red-flags, however, because they themselves don't cause disaster holes. At worst from them, you should be able to play balls back to the fairway without serious damage.

5.2.3 Backspin may not save you

Only high-backspin shots with almost vertical landing angles have a chance to stop on very hard greens. Normal soft greens allow balls to penetrate into the green surface. This penetration leaves a pitch-mark and helps stop the forward momentum of the ball, after which backspin can more readily take effect.

But escape shots rarely have much backspin. When your shot from trouble faces a hard green, a good choice may be to play a bump-and-run type shot short of the green, or to a position which leaves the ball below the flag stick. This would make the next chip and/or putt an uphill shot to this red-flag firm green.

Remember, it's not always easy to put enough backspin on the ball, to fly it to a firm green and get it stopped somewhere near the flagstick, even from good lies on level terrain. Launching shots high with lots of backspin helps this situation. Unfortunately, high shots with lots of backspin won't often be possible from trouble lies.

You should also be aware backspin becomes effective only after balls establish solid contact with the surface of the green. Even shots endowed with plentiful backspin will bounce hard several times on hard greens before establishing roll contact with the surface.

The net effect of all this is: be aware of the moisture content and surface firmness of the greens each round you play. When you play on greens which don't leave pitch marks, beware of playing low-spin shots from trouble to them. Get your red-flags up on all trouble shots under these conditions, and plan on shots not stopping as fast as normal.

5.3 Red-Flags for Slopes

One of the greatest golf courses in the world is Pinehurst #2, located in North Carolina. The design features of #2 contain more red-flag landing areas on and around the greens, which are not-recognized as red-flag areas by golfers, than any course I've ever seen. The surrounds of many greens are contoured to allow all but the best-struck shots to dribble off and away from the putting surface, into extremely difficult chipping or putting positions. While Pinehurst #2's greens aren't surrounded by water, canyons or obvious disaster-pit jungles, and most don't even appear to be elevated, red-flag landing areas for incoming shots create more 8's, 9's, and 10's than anyone would imagine (Figure 5.3.0.1).

This design masterpiece was the creation of Donald Ross, who lived by, played, and studied the course for over twenty years of his life. I can imagine Ross, a good player himself, standing on greens in the evening looking back at the fairways and roughs, planning how to create red-flag landing areas without them being obvious. I'm sure he enjoyed anticipating the non-red-flag equipped golfers, blissfully unaware of what was about to happen to their shots, as they flew, bounced and rolled into disaster scoring situations around and behind his beloved greens.

5.3.0.1

5.3.1 Generic slope effects

Most golfers don't understand how slope can affect the bounce and roll of a ball. Stay with me for a minute here. I'm not going to get too technical, but you need to know how slopes affect your game, especially because these effects are magnified when they combine with shots hit from trouble.

Slopes affect balls rolling up and down hill differently. It is not a case of what you lose rolling uphill equals what you gain rolling downhill, as your intuition might tell you. To see what I mean look at the example of how a ball with a given reference speed rolls 13 feet on level ground (Figure 5.3.1.1). If you tilt the ground (like the back of hole #15 green at Bethpage Black shown in Figure 5.3.1.2) and roll this same ball at the same speed up the slope, it will roll only 7 feet (less than 50% shorter). If you then turn and roll the same ball with the same speed down the same slope, it will roll 42 feet (over 300% farther)!

The slope-roll rule is: balls gain more distance rolling down a hill ... than they lose rolling up it.

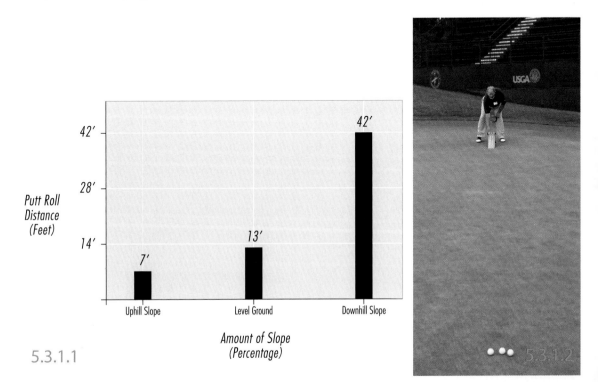

5.3.1.1

5.3.1.2

With regard to how balls bounce, slopes have a different (but again possibly deleterious) effect on a golfer's sensibility. To understand this, let's start with level ground (assume hard ground, so bounce is expected). When a drive lands on a level fairway at a 45-degree angle, it bounces forward at the same angle of 45-degrees (both angles measured from the local perpendicular) as seen in Figure 5.3.1.3A).

The slope-bounce rule is: the angle of incidence equals the angle of reflection. This rule sounds reasonable but its result is not what some golfers expect. It means if the same incoming drive lands on a 15-degree slope it will bounce up at a 75-degree angle, and not roll nearly as far. When the slope changes 15-degrees, the bounce angle changes 30-degrees (twice as much, Figure 5.3.1.3B). That's why balls bouncing off sloped surfaces catch many golfers by surprise.

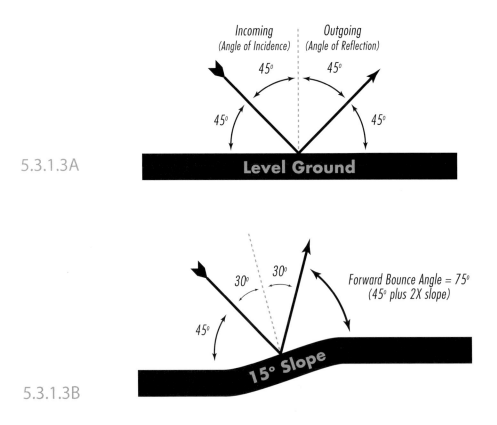

Incoming
(Angle of Incidence)

Outgoing
(Angle of Reflection)

45°   45°

45°   45°

5.3.1.3A

Level Ground

30°   30°

Forward Bounce Angle = 75°
(45° plus 2X slope)

45°

15° Slope

5.3.1.3B

5.3.2 Down slopes are worse than up slopes

The effect of balls hitting down slopes is they kick farther forward than golfers expect them to. This effect gets even worse when a slope running away from the incoming shot direction encounters a trouble shot, which has little or no backspin. In this case, the down slope becomes a disastrous (red-flag) landing area. Just imagine: a low-spinning ball from trouble lands on a firm down slope. The result looks like a scared rabbit; it runs as fast as it can … and will not stop … until it finds a briar patch to hide in!

The slope on the left of the 8th hole of Pinehurst #2 is a red-flag landing area. The last 12 feet on this side of the green starts to slope down the hill, and creates problems for shots coming in from either side of the green. You can see the result of a red flag chipputt up the slope to the pin, in Figure 5.3.2.1. Just imagine what pitching or chipping is like from the other (right) side of the green (just past the pin the slope starts running straight away from the shot, and down this hill to where I'm standing).

5.3.2.1

5.3.3 Firm down slopes can be red-flag specials

Almost all down slopes in play near trouble cause serious problems for golfers. Golf courses have mounds and down slopes all over them, but when a down slope is in play, has trouble below it, and is firm, the problems for golfers multiply to gigantic proportions.

For example, if you find yourself on the back of #9 green at Augusta National like Vijay Singh did (Figure 5.3.3.1), you are above the hole and the (very firm and fast) green is sloping away from you. Even with incredible red-flag touch, this is an extremely difficult shot. Great players sometimes roll such shots down into bunkers (or in the case of the 9th green at Augusta, the shots sometimes roll 70 yards back down the fairway).

5.3.3.1   **A different kind of problem occurs when the lay-up** area for the second shot of a par-5 hole slopes gently down into a pond. This situation becomes a red-flag area immediately upon its turf becoming firm. A similar phenomenon (balls running too far) occurs on greens which slope away from incoming shot directions. Such holes become extremely difficult when the greens get firm, and is the reason you don't see many holes of this design in the game today.

Most greens are designed to slope toward incoming shots to help golfers get their shots stopped. A few with more significant slopes can also become brutally difficult to play. Such a green is the 17th of Valderrama Golf Club, host of the 2000 World Golf Championship (Figure 5.3.3.2). If you saw Tiger Woods score 7 on that hole, after hitting 7 essentially perfect shots, you understand how a fast green sloped down to water can be considered a red-flag opportunity for disasters. Several other players encountered disasters at this hole also, validating its all-world red-flag status (see synopsis next page).

DISASTERS AT VALDERRAMA #17 (536-YARD PAR 5)

-1999 WGC – American Express Championship (Final Round):

-Tiger Woods made an 8 and still won in a playoff
-Bogeys (6) for Sergio Garcia and Stewart Cink cost them $41,000 each in earnings
-Tom Lehman made an 8 on his way to a final-round 80.
-Colin Montgomerie, Mike Weir, John Huston, Steve Pate, Jeff Maggert made 7
-Notah Begay III and Brent Geiberger made 8
-Loren Roberts, Thomas Bjorn and Craig Spence made 9
-David Frost made 10

Other Disasters during that week:

-Bob Estes made 7 in rounds 1 and 3 and still finished T-11

-SIDENOTE: Nick Price (T-4) made par on the hole in all 4 rounds

-2000 WGC – American Express Championship:

-Two back of eventual winner- Mike Weir, Tiger Woods makes 7 at #17 in the final round and loses by 4 shots. Woods found water 3 times (in rounds 1, 2 and 4)
-Nick Price, one shot out of the lead, makes 8 (two balls in the water) in the final round to eventually lose by 4 shots to Mike Weir.
-Eventual winner Weir made a triple-bogey 8 in the second round. (He eagled in round 1, birdied in round 3 and made par in the final round.)
-Mark Calcavecchia and Hidemichi Tanaka also fell out of contention with double-bogey 7.
-Despite disaster scores, the hole averaged 4.817, fourth easiest during the tournament, further emphasizing the importance of red flag awareness.

5.4 Red-Flags for Things You Don't Often Try

There are places on most golf courses where players seldom hit shots. Any time you get into one of those, and have never tried to play from there before (and certainly never practiced from there), you may have trouble executing the shot successfully. When poor execution of a new shot will get you into serious trouble, it should cause a red-flag alert within you.

There are also times when you simply must avoid three putting, even when the percentages say you will probably have difficulty doing so. In golf it often seems to count for more than the one stroke between two putts and three. A three putt can change the momentum of your round, and turn a bad hole into a disaster. Not three putting can also save you from stress on the next hole, when you hit a "less-than-desirable" shot and feel you haven't already wasted too many strokes. Not three putting can help keep your Damage Control Mentality (Chapter 6) intact.

5.4.1 Cut-lobs, bump and runs, high backspin pinch shots

I've been urging golfers to play around and have fun practicing the cut-lob shot for the last 30 years. It's an oft-required shot in golf, but many golfers still don't play with it, and most never practice it. If this description fits you, a cut-lob shot probably warrants your red-flag attention. If you practice it a few times (we have a new way for you to try this without threatening the health of fellow golfers in Chapter 7), you'll find it actually has a nice margin for error. The harder you hit the shot the higher it flies, but the distance it carries doesn't change that much (Figure 5.4.1.1).

5.4.1.1

Bump and run shots are easy to hit, but difficult to judge. Early in my career I was watching and admiring the bump and run work of my good friend Ben Crenshaw (Figure 5.4.1.2). I asked him how he got so good at the shot, as I didn't see any special technique in his hands or swing. To quote Ben (as he looked at me in his own quiet and uniquely honest way and smiled as he said simply): "I've done it a lot!"

Since then I've thought about what he said, and added a thought. Only 50 years ago greens were as slow as fairways are now. This should make bump and running almost like putting back then, and look how well they used to putt. My conclusion: Ben was exactly on target. Practice this shot enough and you can get good at it too. Then you can take the red-flag off it!

5.4.1.2

Pinching a ball to get maximum backspin is a shot most golfers don't have, and don't know how to get. (Of course they haven't practiced it, no one practices what they don't know how to practice.) I caution you against using it, and put a red-flag on it, because it probably won't work from trouble anyway.

The primary requirements for creating spin are a glancing blow, clean contact between your clubface and ball, great grooves in your clubface, and acceleration past impact. From trouble lies, few golfers can produce any, let alone all, of these.

It's risky to use a glancing blow from a bad lie, as there is usually too much stuff around the ball for clean contact. Even if you could accomplish both clean contact and a glancing strike, how many golfers have great grooves and accelerate their clubs past impact? Not many. I hope you get the message: Your red-flag should pop-up any time backspin is required to stop a shot from trouble.

5.4.2 Red-flags for abrupt terraces and level changes

Pelz Golf Institute research shows putts (of 20-25-ft length) which traverse an abrupt level change (terrace) of more than 6-inches are 10-times less likely to be made, and 3-times more likely to be three-putted, than level putts of the same length. Our testing also shows golfers make more than twice as many putts up or down the same elevation changes, if the transition slope is smooth. It is clear golfers don't read the break in terraced greens very well, and even though you haven't seen the data, believe it (Figure 5.4.2.1).

Serious practice is needed to develop touch for the effects of terraces on greens. There is no doubt: sharp terraces deserve red-flag attention whenever you putt up or down over them. The sharper the terrace, and the greater the elevation it traverses, the more dangerous it is. The ultimate terrace is the false front leading into the "Valley of Sin" at the 18th green of the legendary Old Course at St. Andrews Golf Club (Figure 5.4.2.2).

5.4.2.1

1) 20 to 25-foot putts traversing a level change (terrace) of more than 6-inches are 10-times less likely to be made; 2) Putts over the same terrace are 3-times more likely to be three-putted, than level putts of the same length

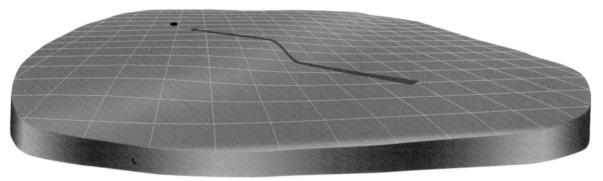

5.4.2.2

5.4.3 Longer shots than you practice

The longer the putt, the more likely it is to be left short of the cup. Do you know why? It's not like golfers couldn't get their putts to the hole if they wanted to. They have plenty of strength and power to get them there, but they don't (as shown in Figure 5.4.3.1). This data comes from mid-handicap (15 to 25) players, but data for pros shows the same trend (pros don't leave the putts as far short).

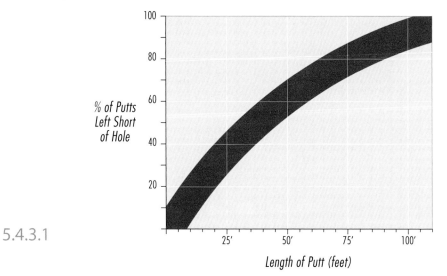

5.4.3.1

% of Putts Left Short of Hole (vertical axis) — *Length of Putt (feet)* (horizontal axis)

The same effect is true for long chip shots (the longer the shot, the more are left short), and there is a good reason for both phenomena. The reason is that golfers always plan the length and intensity of their swings assuming they will hit shots solidly. The longer the swing, however, the less solidly they actually hit these shots.

Imagine then how often players leave extra-long chips and putts short, when they're longer than they've ever tried before. It approaches 100%. In spite of knowing this fact, look how lucky I got at the 18th green at the fabulous new Pete Dye designed Whistling Straits course in Kohler, Wisconsin, before the 2004 PGA Championship (Figure 5.4.3.2).

I want to point out, you're looking at my second attempt at a 206 foot putt, which happened to luck into the hole. They tell me it's the longest putt ever holed on television (if you know of a longer one, please e-mail the details to us at comments@pelzgolf.com). Now look closer, and you'll see my first try, no less than 50-feet short of the hole.

A first putt of 50-feet is a long putt. But to leave yourself a second putt from 50-feet is unheard of. And yes, knowing the probability of leaving long putts short, in front of a world-wide TV audience on the Golf Channel, I left my first putt 50-feet short. I had never tried a putt that long before, and had absolutely no idea of how hard to hit it.

This is why longer shots than you have ever tried before, need a red-flag alert. You'll need all the red-flag touch alertness you can muster, every time you face one.

5.4.3.2

5.5 Red-Flags for Green Speed

The rolling speed of balls on greens is an important and dynamic part of the game of golf. The faster the green speed, the more putts break as they roll to the hole, the farther balls roll before they stop, and the more red-flag touch it takes to control the stopping point of chips and pitches, especially from trouble lies.

The definition of green speed is the distance a golf ball will roll on a perfectly flat green surface, given an initial reference speed. When a ball rolls an average of 8-feet, 10-feet or 12-feet after being given this reference speed, the green has a green speed of 8, 10, and 12 respectively.

5.5.1 Downhill shots get red-flags when green-speeds exceed 10

Downhill chips, pitches and putts are always more difficult to roll at the correct speed to stop near the hole than uphill or cross hill shots. This effect occurs because balls gain more speed rolling down a hill than they lose rolling up it. This difference causes mistakes in starting speeds to be emphasized more for shots going downhill than up. The result: golfer's speed mistakes are magnified on downhill shots, minimized on uphillers.

When you face a downhill putt, especially on a green with a green-speed of 10-feet or greater, be on the alert: forget about your line and focus all of your attention on rolling the ball the proper speed to stop near the hole.

5.5.2 Difficulty increases exponentially at speeds above 11

Faster is not necessarily better, but faster is always more difficult on sloping green surfaces. Modern greens keep getting faster, and when green speed exceeds 11 feet, ordinarily simple shots on mild slopes get really dangerous, warranting red-flags. Beware of green-speed when visiting courses you are unfamiliar with, and keep your red-flag alert system at full attention if you visit what you hear are some of the fastest greens around. On the other hand, if you haven't ever experienced putting on or playing into really fast greens, you should seek them out and do so just for the thrill.

As an example of where difficulty really starts to explode, I can show you a test I ran at Pinehurst #2 before the 1999 U.S. Open. Pinehurst has a great grounds crew under the direction of Robert Farren and Paul Jett (GCSAA) who allowed me to roll shots on the greens several times. In May, the 9th green was a perfect pussy-cat for chipping and putting, and I chipped 10 shots in a row within two feet of the pin, while the green speed measured 10-feet 6-inches.

Then about three weeks later, just before the tournament, I chipped three shots to the same pin for a Golf Magazine article. All three chips were from the same place and were measured to land within three inches of the same spot on the green ... but look where they ended up after the green speed had increased to 11-feet 8-inches (Figure 5.5.2.1: one by the hole, one in the sand, and one rolled back off the green behind where I hit it from). Note: they kept the greens around 12 for the tournament, so imagine how the pros had to play with red-flag touch to score the way they did.

5.5.2.1

5.5.3 Super-fast green speeds above 12

When green speed exceeds 12, essentially all greens become red-flag terrors. Because no greens are flat (water must drain off for the health of the grass), even mildly sloping greens become difficult to play at these speeds, especially when playing from trouble.

A super-fast green can make pitching, chipping and putting reasonable and beautiful (fast greens tend to be smooth, allowing balls to roll in beautifully pure arcs), as long as they slope gently. Add a small amount of additional slope plus contours and undulations, however, and they become very difficult for pros, and terrifying for amateurs (anyone who doesn't have red-flag touch).

On the 16th hole at the Cordillera Mountain Course, at a speed of 12-feet 6-inches, it was difficult to stop this putt from rolling off the green (Figure 5.5.3.1). I had to grip down on the putter shaft to decrease the power I gave the ball. Precision green speed control becomes so very important in this range, as this downhill sliding putt would become unfair (impossible to stop without hitting the hole) with an increase of only a few more inches of additional green-speed.

5.5.3.1

I need to make a counter-point here. You need to understand, super-fast greens can be OK, if they are handled properly. Craig Currier (GCSAA) had his green speed at 14-feet at Beth Page Black on Long Island, NY for the last round of the 2002 U. S. Open. (Note: I'm sure of this speed, because Eddie and I were part of his greens crew the week before and the week during the tournament, and we measured them every morning and evening for Craig, Figure 5.5.3.2).

This is a terrifyingly fast speed, yet not a single player in the field of over 150 of the world's best players complained about the greens being too fast. There were zero complaints because Craig had all his greens rolling consistently at the same speed, and this green speed was appropriate (difficult-but-possible) for the gentle slopes and not-too-wild contours of Beth Page Black.

5.5.3.2

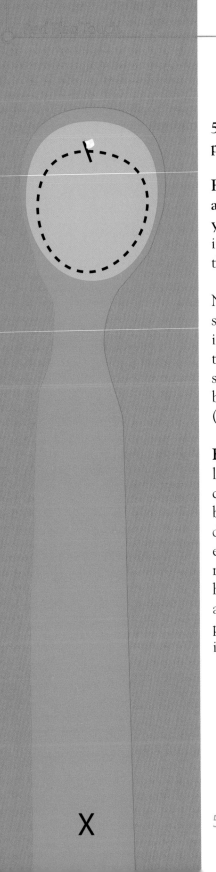

5.5.4 Red-flag conditions create red flag shot patterns

Red flag conditions (slope, green speed, surface and environmental conditions) adversely affect your normal shot patterns. Look at my generic 7 iron shot pattern to a generic green (represented by the black dotted line in figure 5.5.4.1A to the left).

Now look what happens in figure 5.5.4.1B when the same quality of shot (from the same normal lie) flies into and lands on red-flag conditions. Even when the shot has been launched by a reasonably good swing, the resulting size of this shot-pattern (due to ball run-out) becomes enlarged significantly (represented by the orange dotted line).

However, when the lie is bad and the escape swing less than perfect, balls launched into these conditions at the wrong trajectory with low backspin create shot-patterns magnified dramatically over golfers' expectations. At the far end of this spectrum, when the lie is so bad you have no clue as to how or where the ball will go when you hit it, plus you're hitting into a red-flag landing area, you're looking at the ultimate red-flag shot-pattern situation (represented by the dotted red line in Figure 5.5.4.1C)

X

5.5.4.1A

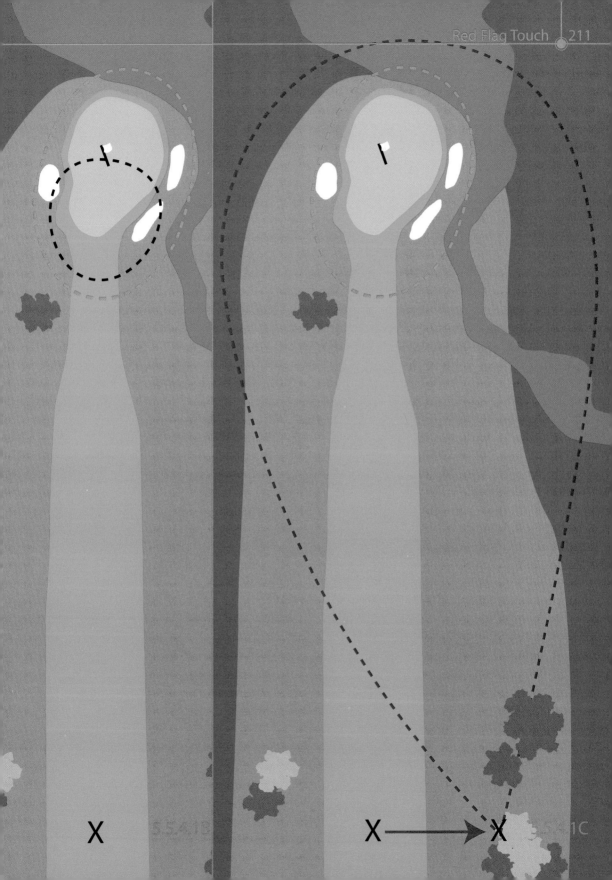

5.6 Pulsating Red-Flags for Combinations

If there is a way to create extra-special red-flag alerts with extended flag poles, glowing or pulsating red-flags, or redder than red colors, it should be used when golfers face the combination of firm and fast conditions, on sloping and undulating golf courses. When these attributes are all combined in landing areas for incoming shots from trouble lies, the results are nothing short of consistent disaster scoring, unless golfers play with the ultimate amount of red-flag touch.

5.6.1 This combination (firm, fast, undulating) ... perfect for major tournament tests

The Masters Tournament has the formula down perfect. The maintenance staff is well managed, talented, and focused on bringing Augusta National to the peak of conditioning every year for tournament week. The Masters provides players with the perfect challenge (weather permitting): fast fairways, firm fast undulating greens with copious slopes, and sloping approaches to those greens. They tailor the course to provide great difficulty from the center of every fairway, and next to impossible red-flag difficulty (not impossible, but close) from trouble left or right.

A chip shot Ernie Els faced during the last round of the 2004 Masters illustrates Augusta National's red-flag perfection. Els missed the #9 green to the right, with a right front pin position. Attempting to pitch close from this position is a red-flag special, with the ball odds-on to roll off the green and 70-yards down the fairway if he tried to play the shot to the flagstick. Ernie pulled it off, however, playing 25-feet of break on a 30-foot shot hit at perfect speed. He hit an essentially perfect pitch with incredible red-flag touch, in what I would estimate was a one-in-a-hundred shot performance (I'll never forget it).

Pinehurst #2 also gets it right for major tournament week, creating typical red-flag conditions behind the 3rd (Figure 5.6.1.1), 9th, 14th, and 15th greens, and to the left of #8 and right of #18 green. And they make these areas so easy to reach. Simply by playing from the 4-inch Bermuda rough to any back pin position and hitting a very good shot (not great, just very good), a player can find their balls dribbling through red-flag conditions into fire lies in a heartbeat. Then, by not playing conservatively and gambling to save par, it becomes almost like asking for disaster.

5.6.1.1

5.6.2 Shinnecock Hills horror stories

Red-flag conditions can turn into impossible conditions. When a golf course becomes too hard and fast for the slopes of its terrain, balls cannot be stopped from rolling off the greens and even red-flag touch is not enough to deal with it. It's certainly no fun to compete when the conditions are neither fair nor possible, such as occurred during the third and fourth rounds of the 2004 U.S. Open Championship. On those two days, Shinnecock Hills became an unfair place to play the game.

The course played beautifully for the first two rounds, but then a few greens dried out and some became unfair, and un-puttable, on Saturday.

A number of the world's best players putted from behind the cup on the 10th hole at Shinnecock Hills on Sunday (4th round), and rolled their balls about 60 yards down the hill in front of the green. The green was so firm and fast, there was no fair place for a hole location on the putting surface.

Then, the wind blew through out Saturday night. After being cut and prepared Sunday morning, by 11:00 AM several greens were so fast balls would not stay on them. Tournament officials were forced to either stop play or water the greens intermittently (periodically between groups) which they did. Yes, they actually watered the greens before some groups ... but not others ... during U.S. Open tournament play. This created moist greens (probably rolling at speeds of 11, perfect for putting) for some players who played immediately after watering, while others had to play "over-the-top-fast" greens (probably in the 14 to 15 speed range, Figure 5.6.2.1). Unfortunately, for some players, it was not fair.

Shinnecock Hills is a great golf course, one of the best in the world, and I'm not denigrating it (I love the course). I mention these conditions because they happened, they may happen again, and knowing about it may motivate you to develop your red-flag touch for the future. You need to be able to recognize and differentiate between normal, difficult, and red-flag conditions. And in doing this, it helps to realize what lies just beyond super red-flag conditions: the unfair ... then the impossible.

≈ 60 yards

5.6.2.1

5.6.3 Red-flags are good things

The development and internalization of red-flag touch in a golfer has two components. One is the desire to acquire a red-flag system in your brain to pop-up, alerting you of red flag conditions when you face them on the course. This component focuses your learning on the evaluation and prediction of the after-execution behavior of your trouble shots, with your brain on full-alert attention. It also indicates a willingness on your part to play with heightened mental energy when you're in trouble.

The other part is developing the appropriate knowledge and experience from results of red-flag situations, and integrating them into your mind's eye. This allows you to know what escape shots you can play and how to play them, before you try them on the course. Learning this takes developing the five skills of Damage Control, using them in Damage Control practice, and finally experiencing the intricacies of using red-flag touch on the course.

You know, if golf was easy, it wouldn't be as much fun. Red-flag conditions are great for the game. They challenge you, punish you, and thank heaven, reward you on occasion. The great courses of the world aren't just the most beautiful courses. They are also the places which make our red-flags pop up most often (Figure 5.6.3.1). We all enjoy playing well, when we're able to pull it off, under red-flag conditions.

As you learn to be alerted by firm and fast landing areas, slopes which control the direction and distance your shots travel, and green speeds nearing the impossible level, you will be learning red-flag touch. You're developing red-flag touch when you realize your next shot, even if you execute it perfectly, may bounce and roll into disaster. And when you kick your imagination into a new place to deal with such conditions, you'll find the game takes on new excitement and meaning.

When your red-flag touch is good enough, you will have added a whole new dimension to your game. It's thrilling to develop and use red-flag touch; and once you do it, you'll have added another skill to your Damage Control arsenal!

5.6.3.1

To play with Damage Control a golfer needs to learn five skills.
The first four have been detailed in the four previous chapters.
Learning to use those four skills within the Code of Damage
Control is the fifth ... the skill of playing with a Damage Control
Mentality.

Set-up-ology, swing shaping and hand-fire feel are physically
oriented skills involved with executing escape shots. Red-flag touch
is the skill of knowing how trouble shots will behave after they are
launched. The skill of playing with a Damage Control Mentality is

different from all of these: it combines 1) the skill of obtaining the information a golfer needs to play successful shots from trouble, with 2) the skill of using this information to play within the Code of Damage Control.

So strap on your seat belt and get ready for something big. In this chapter, you'll learn about the Damage Controller; golf's ultimate information machine built into a tiny computer. Then you'll see how to develop the mental acuity to apply this information. And finally, you'll begin to combine these two skills into your own Damage Control Mentality.

6.1 How the Damage Controller Works

The damage controller (Figure 6.1.0.1) is an incredibly complex computer in a very small package. It incorporates the visual operations of a camera, sophisticated analysis software programs, storage operations of massive memory chips, math calculations of extreme complexity, and a vast understanding of balls, roll, backspin, slopes, swing forces, energy transfer, aerodynamics: i.e. … the physics of golf.

The Damage Controller integrates these systems (which measure and manipulate the complex interactions of golf), with an intelligence system capable of analyzing situations, making decisions, creating graphics patterns, and even making predictions. At the Pelz Golf Institute, we developed the Damage Controller as we studied what information great golfers need and use to successfully play with Damage Control.

6.1.0.1

In a schematic diagram of the Damage Controller (Figure 6.1.0.2) you see it divides functionally into three distinct sections, controlled by three buttons:

1) The "Lie" sector evaluates the lie of a ball and its surrounds, and makes club and swing selections it believes can be played from these conditions.

2) The "Skill" sector takes the club and swing selections from the "Lie" sector output and calculates the shot-patterns a golfer is likely to produce from them, based on his skill level.

3) The "Target" sector is a statistics and probability calculation center. It takes the shot-pattern prediction from the "Skill" sector and calculates the probability-of-success for the shot by projecting the shot pattern onto the various lies around the shot target area.

6.1.0.2

If you have never seen or used a Damage Controller before, it's quite an amazing thing. It was created in a project designed to develop the ability to scientifically acquire, process and analyze the information a golfer needs to successfully play from trouble. The Damage Controller and its processed information need to be especially complete and accurate when golfers face shots from trouble, because the penalties for not getting things right on trouble shots have direct and serious implications on a golfer's ability to score. I say this based on our study of golfers' performance from troubled lies.

Now let me show you how the Damage Controller works and the information and value it provides.

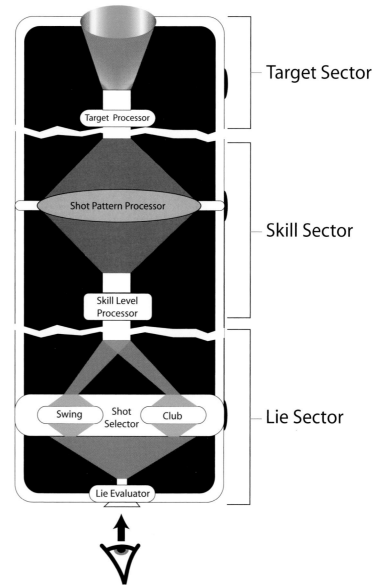

6.1.2 The Lie Sector Sees and Analyzes Conditions

Upon finding a ball in trouble, the golfer turns the Damage Controller on by pushing the lie button. He points it first at the ball, then zooms out to the surrounding area. The Damage Controller examines the lie in detail to evaluate what kind of contact can be made with the ball. It also evaluates what kind of swings can be made considering the conditions (bushes, tree limbs, etc.) surrounding the ball.

With this information, the lie sector creates a prioritized list of shots that can be played from this lie. The lie sector also analyzes and assigns a difficulty to this lie, based on the lie difficulty scale (Figure 6.1.1.1).

Degree of Difficulty	Color
Safe	●
Marginal	○
Frying-Pan Trouble	●
Fire Trouble	●

6.1.1.1

Look at the lie sector operation for a typical frying-pan lie. First, it takes a close-up view of the ball and the area immediately behind (Figure 6.1.1.2). In this case, it looks like good clean contact can be made with the ball. Then as it zooms out, we see the trunk of a tree which might get in the way of the players' swing (Figure 6.1.1.3 next page). It takes just a brief instant for the lie sector to run its analysis and bring up the recommended shot and its difficulty rating onto the screen: Sand wedge, upright 1/2 swing, difficulty = 6 (Figure 6.1.1.4 following page).

6.1.1.2

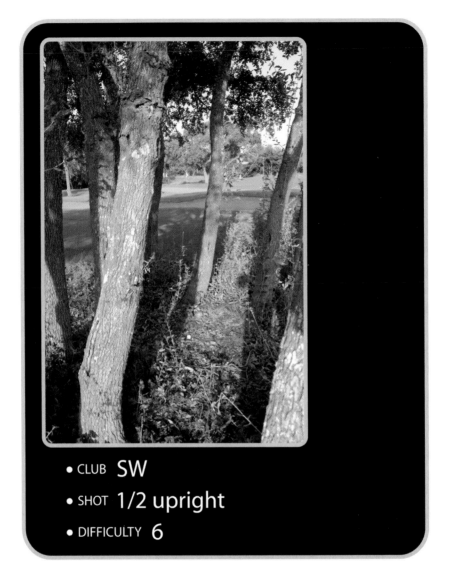

- CLUB **SW**
- SHOT **1/2 upright**
- DIFFICULTY **6**

6.1.1.4

Notice how you see both the shot recommendation and difficulty evaluation in the bottom left corner of the Damage Controller screen. The difficulty rating helps the golfer to be aware of how difficult the recommended shot will be to play.

The "job" of the lie sector is to correctly choose the best club and swing (shot) to use in escaping from trouble, and to advise the golfer how difficult the shot will be to execute. These results are important to the golfer, because a mistake in assessing what club to use, how cleanly club-to-ball contact can be made, or the difficulty of the shot can have disastrous consequences on shots from trouble lies.

6.1.2 The Skill Sector Calculates Shot-Patterns

Upon pushing the skill button, the skill sector instantly merges its memory files for the skill of the golfer with the recommended shot difficulty, to create a shot-pattern the golfer is likely to produce in this situation. The shot-pattern is then displayed on the Damage-Controller screen, so the golfer can see its size and shape (as if on a generic open fairway, Figure 6.1.2.1). Please note: this shot-pattern is completely unique to the golfer whose skills have been programmed into the Damage Controller.

The "job" of the Skill Sector is to accurately assess the likely size and shape of the shot-pattern which will be produced by this particular golfer from the lie in question. If the golfer doesn't want to hit the recommended shot for any reason, he pushes the skill button again to cycle through a prioritized shot list. The Damage Controller shows him a corresponding shot pattern for each shot considered.

The Damage Controller is full of golfer specific data and information, and always selects the best shot for the trouble situation the golfer finds himself in. In the example shown here, we'll go with its wedge shot recommendation.

6.1.2.1

6.1.3 The Target Sector Calculates Odds and Statistics

As important as picking the correct shot to play from trouble is the process of choosing the optimum target for the shot. When our golfer aims the Damage Controller at his chosen target and depresses the target button, his shot-pattern is overlaid onto the course with a superimposed color spectrum indicating the relative percentage of shots ending up in each of the lie categories (green=safe, yellow=marginal, orange=frying-pan, red=fire). A simultaneous calculation of the odds of the shot ending up in a safe lie (odds of success) also appears on the screen.

Look at the output of the target sector for two different target areas (overview Figure 6.1.3.1) for the frying-pan lie we've been analyzing. First see what happens if the player chooses the flagstick as his target (Target #1). His chance of the shot ending up in a safe lie on the green is 20%. That's a 1-in-5 chance of success, with a large number of shots ending up in the sand, falling down from tree limbs, or running over the green into fire lies. These results (statistics) are indicated by the 20% green spectrum (safe) and large (80%) percentage of yellow, orange and red trouble lies. The safe percentage number is displayed in the upper right of the screen.

6.1.3.1

- CLUB SW
- SHOT 1/2 upright
- DIFFICULTY 6

Target #1

Obviously, when a player chooses a dangerous target, his chances of success will not be high. But look at what happens to this same player when he picks a safer area out to the right and 40 yards short of the green as his target (Target #2). His success rate for a shot into a safe lie in the fairway jumps to 92%. Choosing this target, the only way he can get his next shot into trouble, is to shank it.

Target #2

The operation of the Damage Controller was the same for both of these two target choices, but the results were different because when golfers choose a different target, their chance of success changes. An even better illustration of Damage Controller risk / reward analysis for different target selections is shown on the next 5 pages, as our golfer looks at different plays from a frying-pan lie in the right rough (Figure 6.1.3.2). Note for all figures: same lie; same golfer; same skill level; the only thing changing between four Damage Controller pictures is the target selected by the golfer.

- CLUB SW
- SHOT 1/2 upright
- DIFFICULTY 6

You are a 12-handicapper whose drive leaked into the right rough (Figure 6.1.3.2, ball at bottom-center of photo). Your lie is not too bad, but a bush is at the right edge of your direct line to the flagstick. The green is shaped like an inverted L, closer on the front left. The flagstick is farther away (120-yards) on the back right, and serious trouble is everywhere short, right, and long.

Should you play aggressively at the flag, or lay-up out to the left? You could chip out straight left and be completely safe, but that costs one full shot, and you want badly to save par. Let's see what the Damage Controller says about playing this next shot.

6.1.3.2- Overview

Ball

What if you go for the pin?

- CLUB **9-iron**
- SHOT **full cut**
- DIFFICULTY **7**

Play 10 yards left of the flag?

40

- CLUB **PW**
- SHOT **full**
- DIFFICULTY **5**

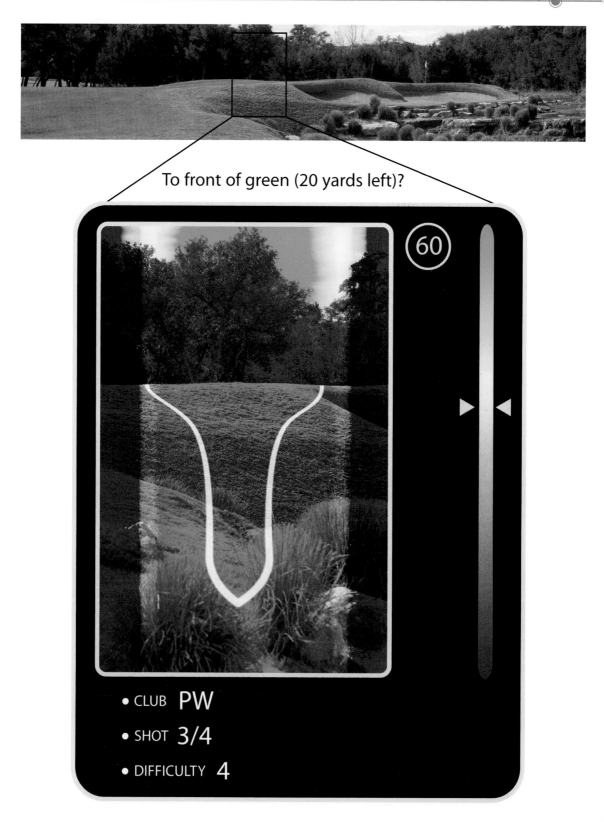

To front of green (20 yards left)?

60

- CLUB PW
- SHOT 3/4
- DIFFICULTY 4

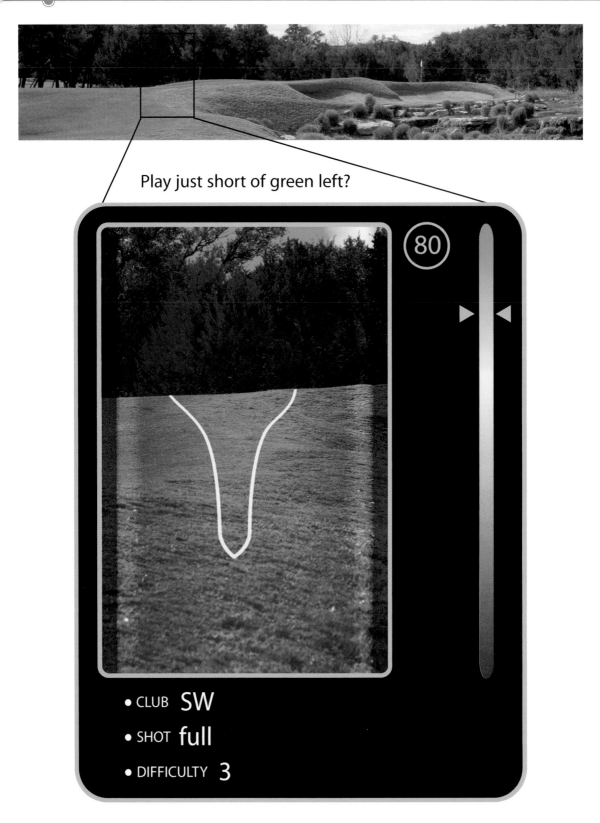

Play just short of green left?

- CLUB SW
- SHOT full
- DIFFICULTY 3

As you can see, the "job" of the target sector is to give the golfer a visual image of his shot-pattern, along with a color spectrum indicating the lies (and safe percentage) of where those shots will end up. This is the output of the Damage Controller; the shot, its difficulty, and the reality of the golfer's chances for every potential target. By comparing different available targets, and seeing his probable results change, a golfer can choose his own destiny. It gives him the information he needs to play, or not to play, with Damage Control.

6.1.4 The Ultimate Information

The patterns into which shots are likely to fly, and the odds of success vs. failure, comprise the information a golfer needs to make an intelligent decision about what shot to hit, where to aim and how to play from trouble. After several years of study, we (Pelz Golf Institute) finally understand what this information is, and how it must be processed, to allow a golfer to play with Damage Control. You've now seen and understand this also.

The Damage Controller takes in information, processes it, and presents probable results to the golfer. It doesn't swing clubs and it doesn't hit shots. It only provides accurate information in the form of shots, difficulty ratings, shot-patterns, and odds of success to the golfer. The golfer can then make his or her decisions, and play the shot.

This is exactly what every golfer needs to avoid disaster holes. Look at how simple the Damage Controller makes playing from trouble. Imagine you drove a ball off to the right into the weeds. You find your ball, point your Damage Controller at it, and click-click-click. Almost instantaneously you see the shot you should play, your projected shot-pattern, and the statistics of where your shots will likely fly.

As you look around to select your target, you aim the Damage Controller at the flagstick (or your most aggressive possible target) and see your chances of success. If the screen tells you this is safe to 90% odds or better (mostly green on the screen), your decision is made. Go for it. You know this is the smartest and best decision for your game and score.

On the other hand, if the screen is filled with lots of red and a less than 10% chance of success, move the Damage Controller to look at a less aggressive target. Let it re-evaluate your odds. Do this until you find your ideal situation; a shot you can play … to the most aggressive target which gives you a 90% or better success rating, a target area surrounded by lots of green.

The Damage Controller is not perfect. It provides you with the relative odds of success for a shot and target within the Code of Damage Control (detailed in Section 6.2.3 below). It can predict results within reasonable tolerances, but will never be 100% perfect, because it deals with humans who are not 100% perfect.

To give you an example; I was watching Johnny Miller, U.S. Open winner and perhaps the best iron player I've ever seen. He was playing his second shot to the 16th green while leading a tournament at Pebble Beach. After a perfect drive, from a perfect lie, he hit a perfect shank deep into the weeds behind a tree on the right. Even though the odds of Johnny playing that shot safely were in excess of 99.9%, he shanked it. His body performed a one-in-ten-thousand bad move. It happens.

Always remember: Although some golfers are awesome … everyone is human … and no one is perfect.

6.2 Two Parts of Damage Control Mentality

Having the skill to gather and analyze the information needed to play from trouble (playing with a Damage Controller) is one component of a Damage Control Mentality. Having the knowledge, mental ability and emotional control to use this information properly is the other. Having the combination of both these skills is what gives a golfer a Damage Control Mentality.

6.2.1 Playing with the Damage Controller.

You now understand how the Damage Controller works and the information it provides. Let's assume for the rest of this section you could afford to buy a Damage-Controller today, and it was programmed perfectly for you and your game. Do you know how, and do you have the emotional control on the golf course, to use the information it would give you?

If you do, this is what would happen: by playing all trouble shots with the clubs, swings, and 90% safe targets recommended, in only 5% of those cases would you again end up in frying-pan or fire lies (the other being 90% safe and 5% marginal lies). If you then played those (5%) follow-on trouble shots according to Damage-Controller recommendations, you would experience having a disaster hole only once in every few hundred trouble situations.

This means instead of encountering two or three disaster holes every round (as you currently experience), you would experience perhaps one disaster every 15 or so rounds.

This would be your experience from playing the shots recommended by the Damage Controller, and aiming at targets of 90% or higher safe success rating. Wouldn't that make playing from trouble simple? Just find your ball, click-click-click the three buttons, and let the Damage-Controller tell you where to aim. Voila, you're playing with Damage Control, and no more disaster scores. This sounds easy, but it's not. As in so many aspects of life, saying things is easy, but doing them is not always so. Following the advice of anyone all the time, even a Damage Controller you know is giving you accurate advice, is not always easy in the heat of battle, on the course, under all conditions, in all situations!

6.2.2 Take a Leap ... Get a Skill

Having a Damage Controller doesn't necessarily give you a Damage Control Mentality. Because the information it provides won't help you unless you use it properly. I know this seems obvious, but it's a truth many golfers ignore: having information is useless if you don't know how, or have the mental and emotional control, to use it.

Being aware of information ... and using it ... are two different things. In Damage Control the move from having information to being able to use it requires a commitment to trust that the information will work. This requires a leap of human judgment, plus handling human emotions not related to logic. No computer programs can be written, no logic systems developed to accomplish this move. This leap acts as a bridge, connecting information with its useful application.

For golf and Damage Control this commitment bridge involves the mental intellect and emotional control to apply intelligent judgment without emotion or ego to Damage-Controller information. Having the skill of using intelligent judgment ... the second component of a Damage-Control-Mentality ... is a skill vital to Damage Control. (Note: by "intelligent" we mean "statistically-accurate" judgment).

The fact is; giving Damage Controller information to golfers often does absolutely no good. I've tried it. It doesn't always work because the skill of using good judgment when in trouble is missing in many golfers. It's not that they aren't intelligent enough to do so. It's a problem of either:

1) Not having the first four skills of Damage Control
2) A lack of awareness of Damage Controller information
3) Never being trained to evaluate risk/reward odds of shots from trouble, or
4) As a result of 1, 2, and 3, playing golf according to their emotions, pressures of the moment, and ego.

The truth is many golfers never imagine the realities of what their shot-patterns might look like, have never considered their probabilities of reward vs. risk when aiming at targets, and seldom if ever let statistics affect their judgment on shots from trouble!

A typical example of poor judgment occurs when a golfer in frying-pan trouble wants badly to save par. This golfer looks at the Damage-Controller's recommendation to hit a wedge out to a safe area 20-yards short of the green (green path in Figure 6.2.2.2). But he knows he can fly an 8-iron on the green, if he catches it really well (red path).

He knows the Damage-Controller's safe route is probably the smarter, higher-percentage way to play. It requires only a reasonable pitch from short of the green, plus a five or 10-foot putt to save par. But he also knows he can, he possibly-can, hit that 8-iron shot on the green. He really wants this par, and he really wants to hit that 8-iron onto the green, so he can simply two-putt for it.

In this situation, golfers go for it nine times out of 10. And in those nine times they make two pars, two bogeys, two doubles and three triple bogeys (Figure 6.2.2.3).

6.2.2.3 - The Percentages of Damage Control Scoring

-10 times "Damage Control" average score = 4.5

-10 times "Go For It" average score = 5.5

So how can golfers develop the skill of using intelligent judgment in their trouble games? It sounds difficult doesn't it? But it's not really.

It's like learning about a diet that will keep weight off, which also sounds like something you can actually live with and accomplish. Before you can benefit from it, you've got to commit to trying it! I don't want you to commit to Damage Control because Dave Pelz says it works. I want you to commit to it because you understand what this book is telling you about your game, you recognize the disaster score scenario in your past play, and you understand how Damage Control will improve your ability to shoot lower scores.

Learning to use good judgment in your game involves knowledge. You must understand if it's better on average, then it's better more often than it's worse. You must recognize how the targets you choose from trouble, and the odds of success on shots hit to them, determine your scores. You must believe in the statistics which say you'll score better by escaping before you recover from trouble, than by trying hero shots … even when your gut tells you to go for it.

The skill of using intelligent judgment can be learned experientially in Damage Control practice rounds. As you become aware of your shot patterns and how your target choices affect your results (detailed in Chapter 7), your Damage Control judgment will improve. Then you need mental strength, discipline, and emotional control … to believe in … and commit to … Damage Control. You need to take the leap of using this knowledge on the course, in real rounds which count for score. It works, and will save you 2 to 5 strokes per round, but you need to believe it enough to try it, and prove it to yourself!

The Second Ball

If you sometimes have an insanely strong desire to try risky or dangerous shots, I have an idea for you. Play your real ball with Damage Control first, then try going for it, hitting dangerous shots with a second ball just for the thrill of it. This way if you hit the shot successfully, it's fun. If it fails, it doesn't ruin your score.

Playing with a second ball in your pocket is also beneficial to your future, because you'll sub-consciously learn how often your "hero" shots turn out to collect the risk penalty, instead of the reward you were looking for (remember: to collect the reward after hitting a great shot from trouble, you still have to make the next putt).

6.2.3 The Code of Damage Control.

Once you have the 5 skills of Damage Control, playing with Damage Control means applying those 5 skills within the Code of Damage Control (Figure 6.2.3.1), whenever your ball finds trouble.

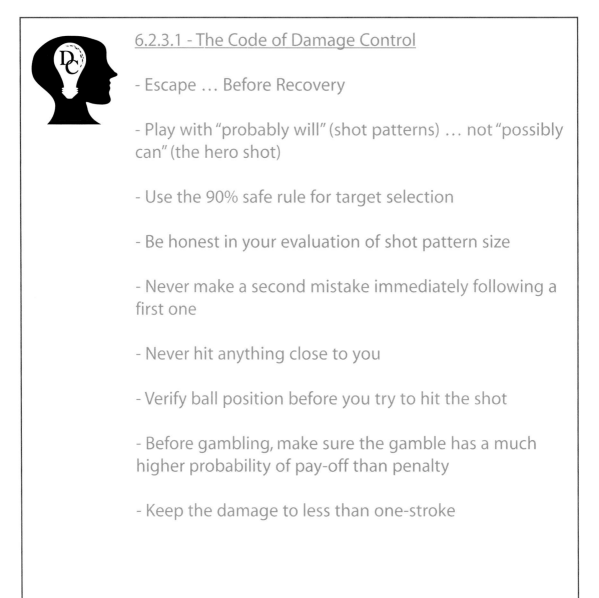

<u>6.2.3.1 - The Code of Damage Control</u>

- Escape … Before Recovery

- Play with "probably will" (shot patterns) … not "possibly can" (the hero shot)

- Use the 90% safe rule for target selection

- Be honest in your evaluation of shot pattern size

- Never make a second mistake immediately following a first one

- Never hit anything close to you

- Verify ball position before you try to hit the shot

- Before gambling, make sure the gamble has a much higher probability of pay-off than penalty

- Keep the damage to less than one-stroke

Escape … before you recover. The concept of recovering from trouble is not good, because it leads to frequent disaster scores. Escaping from trouble first, then trying to recover (by a great wedge shot, or holing a putt) without losing a stroke to your score is a better way to play. The numbers are why I say this. Just look: If you escape on the first shot over 90% of the time, then get the ball up and down 40 to 60% of the time, you average losing only a little over half a shot per encounter with trouble. These are not unrealistic numbers (many of the PGA Tour players I coach achieve better than this).

Play with probably will … not possibly can. You probably will hit one of the shots out of your shot-pattern each time you play from trouble. If however you consistently try shots that you possibly-can-but-probably-won't hit, you will continue to suffer disaster scores and disaster holes regularly, almost every round you play.

If 90% of your shots from trouble end up in safe lies, you can control the damage to your scores. This is the 90% rule. It means (by a simple progression of statistics and percentages) you will encounter a disaster hole only once every 15 or 20 rounds, instead of several times in each round, as so many golfers do.

Learn the size and shape of your shot-patterns. This is easy to accomplish (as you will see in Chapter 7.4) by creating "quick-view" shot-patterns, which give you snap shots of your real skill and your real shot-patterns from any particular lie. By playing Damage Control practice rounds over a period of time, and accumulating multiple quick-view shot-patterns, you'll learn the realities of your trouble game.

Never make a second mistake immediately following a first one. Even following the 90% rule, 10% of your escape shots from trouble are going to end up in marginal, frying-pan, or fire trouble. Assuming 5% end up in frying-pan or fire lies, these are the shots you cannot afford to hit poorly. For the 5% of the times this happens to you, you should become very conservative and use the simplest of shots to super-safe targets on your second escape attempts. In other words, if you don't escape on the first try, make absolutely certain you do on the second.

Many of the golfers in our disaster score study said their worst three swings of the day came in succession (leading to a double-digit disaster hole). They frequently referred to their "bad things come in threes" superstition as an excuse.

The truth is an additional bad swing following a first is easy to make from troubled lies because:

1) Trouble lies and stances are much more difficult to swing from than are normal lies on level terrain;

2) Golfers tend to be mad or embarrassed after making a bad swing, and sometimes flub the next one because of rushing to "get out of here quickly."

Always buckle down after a bad shot gets you into, or fails to get you out of, trouble. Don't try a risky recovery shot to save face or to avoid any possibility of losing an additional stroke; instead play safely out with a good swing and accept that you might lose another stroke (or not if you recover well and are lucky).

The rule is: never try to make a perfect swing (that needs to be perfect to avoid trouble) after a bad swing. Instead, just make a reasonably good swing to a safe target, then try to recover and one-putt.

Never hit anything close to you. When you hit a rock or a tree or anything close to where you're hitting from, the ball has lots of energy and can bounce anywhere. It may hit you (two shot penalty), rebound into the water (another shot penalty), career out of bounds (two shot penalty), or bounce deeper into the rough, causing you to score who knows what. This is in contrast to hitting something far away from you after the ball has lost most of its energy. In this case, the ball won't bounce far and usually will not cost you additional penalty strokes.

Verify good ball position. Don't swing at a trouble shot until you know where your swing arc will bottom out from the posture and stance you are in. A Damage Control pre-shot routine which includes this verification is detailed in Chapter 7; don't miss it (learn it and never play from trouble without it).

Before gambling, make sure the gamble has a much higher probability of pay-off than penalty. For shots from trouble, there are always two questions to be answered: 1) If you choose a 50% safe target, how many of the safe shots will you one-putt? 2) Will those one-putts be a greater savings than the loss of strokes encountered by the 50% of the shots which didn't find safety? (Note: I used a 50% safe target choice in this example. For any trouble shot, answer these two questions for the safety percentage of the target you actually choose to hit too).

Keep damage to less than one-stroke.   Believe in averages, statistics, odds, and percentages. All Damage Control asks is: escape to a position better than you would have been in, if you had not hit into trouble in the first place. When you're in trouble, play conservative escapes and depend on good recovery play to save potential stroke loss. This virtually eliminates disaster holes from your score cards and gives your short game the chance to make you a better player.

6.2.4 Damage Control is not Course or Game Management

Damage Control is not about playing safe off the tee or from good lies in the fairway. Damage Control is about playing out of trouble after you're in it, as aggressively as you possibly can, while staying within the Code of Damage Control. It means playing from trouble while avoiding additional trouble lies and without risking penalties. Always play with a positive slant to your Damage Control effort. The closer you get your escape shot to the front of the green, the more likely you are to avoid losing a stroke.

Course management is not Damage Control. Course management has to do with the way the golf course is designed, and the strategy you choose to play it. Each hole was designed by a course architect with a specific play route in mind. Sucker pin positions and overly penal driving areas should be negotiated with care. Play away from serious trouble areas. This is good course management and is highly recommended, but it has nothing to do with Damage Control. No matter how well you manage your way around the golf course, you will still get into trouble, and you'll need to minimize the scoring damage from there.

Game management is not Damage Control either. You can't tell a golfer how to manage his game, if you don't know his skill level or what his most likely misses and shot-patterns look like.

All golfers, even Tour Professionals, should manage their games according to the dictates of their own shot-patterns. They (and you) can change (improve) their shot-patterns over time, and possibly even change their game management as a result. But again, this is game management ... not Damage Control.

6.3 Developing your own Damage Control Mentality

Let's take a quick status update here. By now you know about the five skills of Damage Control (set-up-ology, swing shaping, hand-fire feel, red-flag touch and Damage Control mentality). You also understand what's involved in the two capabilities (attaining information from the Damage Controller and using it with intelligent judgment) which make up Damage Control Mentality.

You've also seen how you must believe in and commit to using Damage Control, to have a chance of developing a Damage Control Mentality. What you haven't yet learned, is how to get a Damage Controller! You know the information it provides is absolutely necessary for playing with Damage Control, but what can you do about getting one?

6.3.1 Can you buy a Damage Controller?

The question is: how can you get the only thing missing ... Damage Controller information ... to complete your Damage Control Mentality? For that matter, knowing how to get a Damage Controller would complete your knowledge of knowing how to get the entire five skills of Damage Control. Can you afford to simply buy a Damage Controller, to complete the package?

I think not. As far as I know there are no Damage Controllers for sale in the whole world. Maybe they're available on some other planet, in some other galaxy in the cosmos, but not here on earth. And mine, the one we've developed at the Pelz Golf Institute, is not for sale. That's for sure.

6.3.2 You Can't afford NOT to get a Damage Controller

I hope by now you understand and appreciate the critical nature of the information the Damage Controller provides to a golfer. I hope you understand its value for making good decisions when playing from trouble. Because of the importance of information to a Damage Control mentality, I say you can't afford to go without a Damage Controller.

You must have one. There is no way out of the need for one. No one can control scoring damage from trouble if they can't look through a Damage Controller and see how bad their lie is, what swings are required, and what shot-patterns they are likely to generate from this situation. No one can minimize damage if they can't see the Damage Controller's odds of success likely for their escape shots.

So you must get a Damage Controller to attain a Damage Control Mentality, which you must develop before you can play with Damage Control. Although I've mentioned several times earlier in the book how you would have to wait to develop and refine your other skills of Damage Control until Chapter 7, I want to discuss how you can get your own Damage Controller now.

6.3.3 Create your own

I created my own Damage Controller and I think you can too. Because I'm nothing special. I've never been really wealthy, I don't have incredible talent, I'm not the sharpest knife in the set, and I don't have special skills you don't have. Fundamentally, this means if I did it, then you can too. Especially if I give you a little help. So, do you want a Damage Controller of your own? Yes? Well … here's how to get it.

Sit back, close your eyes, put one hand on top of your head and concentrate. Press down on your brain (Figure 6.3.3.1) and tell yourself the following; I will forever hereafter designate one-quarter of a cubic inch of my brain to be my Damage Controller.

While your eyes are still closed, also commit to programming your Damage Controller to your skill level and train it in the 5 skills of Damage Control (drills detailed in Chapter 7). You will also send the information (listed on the next page) to it for every trouble situation you encounter in the future:

1) A clear vision of the lie and all trouble around it which could affect your swing or ball contact

2) Your choice of club and swing (a shot) which you believe will allow your ball to escape from the trouble

3) The imagined shot-pattern you will produce with this shot

4) The reaction you imagine the worst and best shots will have after you hit them (worst first, then best)

5) A clear post-shot report (observation) of where the shot actually ends up

That's it. Now open your eyes and smile. You now have a Damage Controller (Figure 6.3.3.2)! More accurately stated … you are now aware you have one. Your Damage Controller is in your head. It's part of your brain, it's yours; it will always be there for you. The truth is, you and all golfers have always had Damage Controllers in your brains.

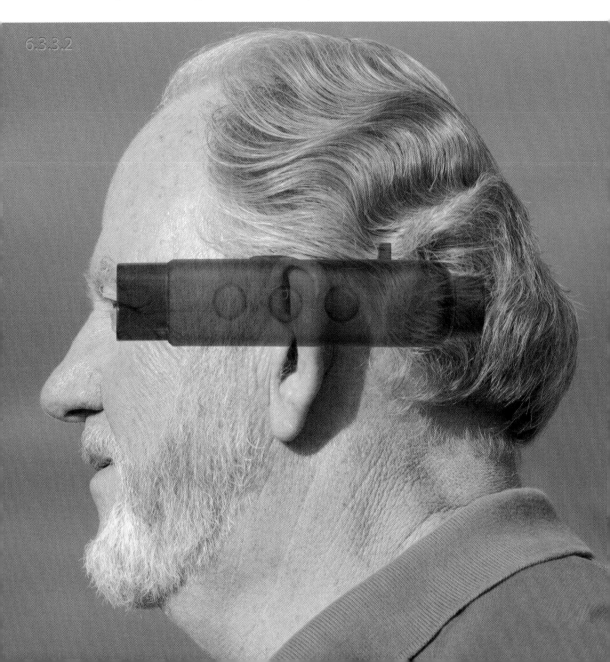

6.3.3.2

My friends Phil Mickelson, Vijay Singh, Steve Elkington, Mike Wier, and Lee Janzen all have Damage Controllers in their heads programmed full of skills, lie information, shot-patterns and probabilities specific to them. That's how they all play with Damage Control, and one of the reasons they've all won Major Championships. Your Damage Controller, and those of most amateurs, might not be very good or useful or valuable because they may have never been programmed with any significant Damage Control information.

Are you surprised … that you already have your own Damage Controller in your head? Or, did you already see this coming? No matter! As long as you now understand and believe, you do have a Damage Controller. Of course, you need to program it if you want it to be worth anything.

The cost of getting a functional Damage Controller in your brain is real. There really is a cost of time (reading this book), practice (in your backyard), and mental engagement (on the golf course during a few Damage Control practice rounds). It will take time to program your Damage Controller to be useful … to allow you to play with Damage Control when it counts … on the course for the rest of your life. But it will be worth it, because it will reward you many times over with lower scores and enjoyment of the game.

6.3.4 You've got it now

You're close now to having a Damage Control Mentality. You've got your Damage Controller in your head, and you've committed (I hope) to develop and use intelligent judgment in your Damage Control game on the course. You might be feeling your Damage Controller is in dire need of some good input information, however, and you're probably right.

But don't worry. Your Damage Controller will function properly once you get the right information programmed into it. After you train it for your physical skills of Damage Control, it will learn from experience how to make good escape swings. Then, as you begin to use those swings, it will begin to notice your shot-patterns from trouble, and store them in your fantastic memory bank.

When you get on the course, it will look at your trouble lies, with all the stuff around your ball, and choose shots with an eye toward their chances of successful escape. It will even look out and estimate what your shot-patterns might look like (Figure 6.3.4.1), as it evaluates different target options within the Code of Damage Control.

6.3.4.1

Will you see the color spectrum and the percentage numbers of my Damage Controller in your vision on course? Probably not ... at least not at first. But your brain (the Damage Controller part of it) will be aware of the essence of danger involved, and your probable odds of success. When you use this information to create a shot which escapes from the trouble you're in, follow it with a good short game recovery shot to avoid losing a stroke on the hole. You'll have merged your Damage Controller with your intelligent (statistically accurate) judgment and played with Damage Control.

 **Please understand: We initially presented the Damage Controller in this book as a mechanical device which could be bought, like a camera or a computer. Our intent in doing this was to focus your attention on the information the Damage Controller provides.**

We didn't want you to worry about how you were supposed to gather and analyze this information. Rather, we wanted you to focus on the use and the value of the information itself. You will see how to program (learn) the information into your Damage Controller in Chapter 7. If we offended you by intimating the Damage Controller isn't part of your brain, we apologize, no offense intended.

6.4 Turn it on

So, now you know. You already have a Damage Controller. You've always had one! Your Damage Controller just isn't efficient yet because you've never programmed it with Damage Control information. In fact, it may have never been turned on before now!

Understand, opening-up your mind to the concepts of Damage Control is one of the main goals of this book. Helping you to understand the five skills of Damage Control and the Code of Damage Control is also big. In the grand scheme of things, to develop a Damage Control Mentality, you must have a small part of your brain devoted to gathering and processing information (Damage Controller), while incorporating intelligent judgment (without emotion and ego).

6.4.1 Your game is … what it is (for now)

There is bad news and good news at this juncture. The bad news is your normal game will never be good enough to keep you out of trouble. You currently may not have the skills or knowledge to play with Damage Control and avoid disaster holes. But the good news is you now know what you have to do to solve this problem: you must finish reading this book, do the drills suggested in Chapter 7, and then use your Damage Control Mentality on the course.

More good news is you can develop Damage Control skills in a heart-beat, relative to the rest of your golf career. Learning Damage Control is simple compared to what you've been trying to learn. Your previous game improvement practice was devoted to improving your normal (safe lie) swings. Keep up this pursuit and I truly wish you improved (smaller) safe lie shot patterns in the future. But, for today, your shot patterns are what they are because really good normal swings are really hard to learn.

Functional Damage Control swings, however, which don't have to be that good, are far easier to learn. Our program for Damage Control takes a different approach to learning them.

Your Damage Controller has been turned off for all the years you've played golf. The concept of teaching Damage Control is new, so you might not know how to position your body on uneven lies or to make flat or upright swings. You probably don't know what your shot-patterns look like from trouble lies. You also may not be aware of the statistical nature of playing shots into safe areas and recovering without losing a stroke in your score. This is all reasonable. After all, you've probably never once in your whole life taken the time to hit 10 shots from a trouble lie just to see were they go (and show yourself a shot-pattern from that kind of trouble).

Although you've hit shots from trouble before, your Damage Controller wasn't switched on to be watching your results at the time, and you weren't aware it would be good to know your shot-pattern shapes. Your brain didn't "imagine" all those shots were forming the shape of your shot-patterns. Also, your set-ups, swings and body motions were probably not yet programmed for Damage Control. All of your previous practice making normal swings from level terrain has done nothing to help you learn to make Damage Control swings from trouble.

Your game is what it is, for now. But just wait. You're getting close to starting to build the new you, the golfer who plays with Damage Control!

6.4.2 Three Steps of Learning Damage Control

It's like a three step ladder you must climb to reach the top performance plateau for your current skill level in the game. This top plateau of optimal performance can be obtained by playing without disaster holes or scores for all 18-holes of almost every round.

I compare this learning process to a ladder, because you need to take the steps in order. You can't go to the second level until you've conquered the first, or the third before the second (Figure 6.4.2.1).

Let me take you through these three steps:

6.4.2.1 - Three Steps of Learning Damage Control

#1: Back yard swing practice with Damage Control balls

#2: On-course practice to determine shot-patterns and red-flag touch

#3: On-course programming of your internal Damage Controller

Step 1 = Learn the first three skills of Damage Control (set-up-ology, swing shaping, hand-fire feel), and get an initial idea of what your shot-patterns look like in your own backyard (details in Chapter 7, Sections 7.1 to 7.4). Simulated trouble lies and Damage Control balls create a great learning environment with good feedback, with convenient practice (with no damage to property or scores) at home.

Step 2 = Learn red-flag touch and develop your shot-pattern recognition in Damage Control-Practice rounds on your local golf course (Chapter 7, Section 7.5). These are rounds in which you don't keep score, or hit shots off each tee. On each hole you simply go straight to the trouble areas you usually get into off the tee (or around the greens), throw down 10 balls, and hit a 10-shot pattern of shots from where they lie.

Step 3 = Play a Damage Control- Supergamble round on your local course, followed by a Damage Control- Supersafe round, both for score! These are normal rounds, except in the Supergamble round every time you play a shot from a trouble lie, you pick a 20% or less target. In the Supersafe round you pick all 90% or greater Supersafe targets. In other words, play these rounds with an overemphasis on Damage Control standards.

Make sure you keep an honest tally of both of your final 18-hole scores. Follow the Code of Damage Control for every trouble shot you face. Then evaluate your scores.

6.4.3 Evaluate (like a Damage Controller) the details of these rounds

There should be no disaster holes or disaster scores on your scorecard for the Supersafe round. There may be several, however, on your Supergamble round. Examine the rounds down to the holes where you encountered serious scoring trouble, and see how many times it was a bad swing vs. a bad target selection which cost you the strokes. Also, examine how often your successful Supergamble recovery shots resulted in the reward of saving shots. There will be a balance point somewhere between a Supersafe and a Supergamble mentality, which is best for scoring for every golfer, based on his or her skill level. The goal is to find that point of balance for your game, enabling your Damage Controller to use it in managing the decisions and choices in future play.

Once you find your balance point, instead of the 2 or 3 disaster holes you used to encounter each round, you should soon be looking at only one really bad hole every 15 or so rounds you play. This kind of improvement will come for sure, but only after you've developed some skills of Damage Control, including a Damage Control Mentality.

Soon, when you look at your scores played after you learned Damage Control, an average of 2 to 5 strokes per round will have disappeared compared to your past history. The 2 to 5 strokes I promised you at the beginning of this book are almost yours.

6.4.4 What's next?

You've now read the difficult parts of this book. If you understand Chapters 2 through 6 (the five skills of Damage Control), you should be ready to learn how to learn these skills. This means reading Chapter 7, the "how-to" section of this book.

In your backyard you will learn to stand, feel, swing, and see how the physical skills of Damage Control work. In Damage Control practice rounds you will learn the procedures and shot patterns of playing with Damage Control, and develop red-flag touch. And by playing a few real rounds with emphasis on Damage Control standards, you'll refine your own Damage Control risk-reward system. It's exciting what all this can do for your scoring, but be patient: the backyard and golf course will wait. Reading Chapter 7 is your next move.

At this point in the book you have a basic understanding of Damage Control. You've read its concepts, seen its skills, and thought about its mentality. But understanding will only take you so far. It's time now to internalize the "feels" of Damage Control into your mind and body.

This can be accomplished in three steps. The first is to learn to make reasonably good escape swings from trouble lies in your backyard. Yes, you read that correctly: You can practice the drills of set-up-ology, swing shaping, and hand-fire feel while hitting special Damage Control practice balls, at home in your own backyard. It's convenient, effective, and the most efficient way to internalize the feelings of these swing skills. We call this step "Take it to the Backyard" (find it by looking for the red-edged pages).

The second step (blue-edged section) is termed "Take it to the Course", where you use the skills learned in your backyard to learn about your shot-patterns and red-flag touch in Damage Control practice rounds on the course.

The final step (green page section) is "Take it to Your Game". This involves fine-tuning your Damage Control Mentality as you return to playing normal golf for score. How you handle trouble in these rounds identifies how your Damage Control mentality should be refined, and where practice should be focused in the future.

Once you accomplish these three steps you will be prepared to avoid disaster scores and shoot lower scores; that is, you will have become a Damage Control player.

7.1 Getting Started

NOTE: This chapter is different from the previous chapters. You should view it as your Damage Control instruction manual. The drills are indexed into three color-coded sections which correspond to the three steps of learning Damage Control. The drills and activities of these three steps are indexed on pages 270 & 271 for easy reference. The drills also reference specific pages in the book which address their specific topics and skills.

7.1.1 Select a Damage Control Practice Area

The first step in learning Damage Control is to find a space in which you can swing safely and hit Damage Control practice balls. These balls (Figure 7.1.1.1) are made and branded Damage Control for us (they're also available under the trade name "Point three" balls, manufactured by Almost Golf Co.). They are very light, have one-third the core rating, and fly only about one third the distance of normal golf balls. Molded with dimple patterns for good aerodynamics, Damage Control balls come off your club like real balls, except they don't fly as far, break windows or dent cars.

Look at the side yard of the Pelz Golf office building (Figure 7.1.1.2). Do you have space in your backyard? Most importantly, this space must be nearby and convenient for you to use, so you don't have to waste time traveling to and from practice. In learning these new skills, you won't care at first where your shots go. In your backyard you turn your attention internally and focus on the swings and feels of Damage Control, with no worries about lost strokes or score. I can't overemphasize how important this is to your long term success in playing with Damage Control.

7.1.2 Gather Materials

You can't just go out back and start swinging however. You need to set-up some learning aids first, to simulate the difficulties of trouble lies and swing obstacles on the golf course. The items you need are shown below in Figure 7.1.2.1 with the corresponding "shopping list" on the next page. Don't worry; gathering up these items for practice will not be a big deal, as they are available from your local Home Depot, Lowes, or home improvement stores (except Damage Control practice balls, which can be ordered directly from www.pelzgolf.com or www.almostgolf.com).

List of Materials

1) Target net (available at sporting goods store)
2) Platform -two 3'x3' 3/4" plywood squares
   -two 3'x3' pieces of artificial turf/outdoor carpet with decent pile (to hold balls when platform is sloped)
   -heavy duty double-sided tape (for attaching carpet to wood)
   -two 10" gate hinges (or any heavy duty hinge or hasp)
3) Two cinder blocks
4) Bag of play sand
5) Fake rock -one can of foam insulation
   -one 1'x2' piece of cardboard
   To make: a) spray foam onto cardboard in a swirling motion
   b) store in out of the way place, wait three days to dry
6) Plastic bucket (to hold water or sand)
7) Boot tray (low lipped plastic tray or lid)
8) Damage Control practice balls (minumum of 10)
9) Fake tree and limb -one 4' 1/2" wooden dowel (one end sharpened)
   -one 5' pool noodle
   -one 5' long, 1" diameter piece of pipe insulation
   -4' piece of heavy copper ground wire (as limb support)
10) Chair (simulating large obstacle)

Please note any of these items can be changed/substituted per availablity and practice area needs. Hand fire feel drills can have mulch, pine needles, peat moss, etc. added to water and/or sand when heavy resistance materials are required. Check our website (www.pelzgolf.com) in the future for further back yard practice area and equipment ideas and suggestions. We would also like to hear from you (email photos, plans, ideas, etc.) regarding the designs and construction of your Damage Control practice area and equipment.

Notice: Danger Warning

Practice at your own risk!

Practicing golf is just as dangerous as playing golf. You can slip from a platform, carpet, block or chair, swing and hit yourself or others, and serious injury can occur. Equipment can be especially dangerous when wet. Please proceed with caution, at your own risk!

7.1.3 Set up your Damage Control Learning Station

Remember – Safety First! Make sure you've oriented you're learning station so no one can walk up behind you without you being aware of them. It's your responsibility to make sure no one ever gets hit or hurt by a swinging golf club. Whether at the golf course or at home, please be careful when swinging a club.

You should also be careful to hit the Damage Control balls away from people. Even though the balls probably won't hurt anyone seriously, I'm sure being hit and surprised by a ball would be irritating and should be avoided. These balls normally fly about 1/3 the distance of a normal golf ball: that's not too far for wedge shots, but if you're practicing irons and woods, they can fly over 100yds.

Look again at our learning station at Pelz Golf with learning aids in use (Figure 7.1.3.1). The backyard of my home is shown in Figure 7.1.3.2. As you can see at Pelz Golf we have lots of room and could hit in virtually any direction. At home I have almost no space, no yard, and must stop anything more than a pitch shot in the net. However, even this confined area is still a great place to practice and learn Damage Control techniques.

As you may have guessed from our Golf Channel shows and Golf Magazine articles, the authors of this book (myself, Eddie Pelz, and Joel Mendelman) are all enthusiastic students of the game (golf nuts). We all have Damage Control practice stations; Eddie's in his large side yard, and in Joel's case inside his apartment (Figure 7.1.3.3ab). As you can see, Joel's set-up doesn't take up much space, so we don't want to hear any excuses from you about not having enough room to learn the skills of Damage Control!

7.1.3.2

7.1.3.3A   7.1.3.3B

7.2 How to Approach Damage Control Shots and Drills: The Damage Control Pre-Shot Routine

The best way to optimize the way you play golf is to optimize your practice. The easy way to make this happen is to be smart enough to practice like you're going to play.

7.2.1 Practice like you play

Every trouble shot you attempt is a new and unique experience. For each new trouble lie you encounter, you will set up in a slightly (sometimes grossly) different way, with your body in a different position from the swings you normally make from safe lies on tees and level fairways. That is why it's important to have a consistent approach to understanding (both physically and intellectually) the specific demands of trouble shots. Each Damage Control drill in your backyard (and every on-course trouble shot) should begin with the Damage Control pre-shot routine. This routine must become a habit, a part of your game for now and in the future. The Pelz Golf Institute recommended Damage Control pre-shot routine proceeds through three steps as follows:

> 1) Check/feel for **body set-up** stability/balance with or without a club (set-up-ology)
> 2) Check obstacles for **swing clearance** and how they affect or interfere with your swing (stutter- step practice swing)
> 3) Check for **final feel and ball position** with a preview swing

Start step 1 (set-up-ology) with or without a club to focus on "feeling" how the set-up position of your body interacts with the lie and terrain of this trouble shot. These feelings will be refined in step 2 (stutter-step practice swing) when you grab the appropriate club and move slowly through nine positions of the swing. As you increase your tempo and move closer to the ball, step 3 (the preview swing) will simulate the swing you actually want to make. This prepares you for the swing feel and balance you will experience and allows you to verify that your ball position is precisely correct. Again, the emphasis in this pre-shot routine is to optimize body and ball position, and your swing feel prior to shot execution. This will be detailed in the rest of this section.

7.2.2 Pre-Shot Routine Step 1: Set-up-ology

Set-up-ology positioning is grouped into three general categories of bodily movement: Spine Angle, Spine Lean and Stance Width. Don't hesitate to re-familiarize yourself with these movements (Chapter 2) as necessary when they are referenced in the drills.

7.2.3 Damage Control Pre-Shot Routine Step 2: Stutter-Step Practice Swing

The next step in the Damage Control pre-shot routine is the stutter-step practice swing. This swing involves a nine position trouble swing (Figure 7.2.3.1) with gradually increasing tempo.

7.2.3.1

Practice Swing #1: Address an imaginary ball close to (about 10-inches) the real ball. Duplicate the set-up and stance you expect to take for the real shot. From this posture execute a swing in which you **stutter-step** through each of the 9 key positions of a swing. As you reach each position, stop and identify if any obstacles will affect you there. Pause momentarily to experience how each swing position "feels." Feel the effort you expend in getting to and holding each position. (Note to self: The greater the effort to attain or hold any position, the more difficult it will be to make the swing through this position in your upcoming real swing).

Practice Swing #2: From the same position (10-inches from the ball) take a second swing in **slow-motion,** through the same 9 positions of swing #1. During the slow-motion swing, concentrate on feeling your body move (as if you had your eyes closed, but don't close them).

Practice Swing #3: Move slightly closer to the ball (same set-up and stance) and take another swing at about **3-quarter speed,** somewhat faster than swing #2. Again feel your body move and your balance requirements for making the swing. Keep this swing smooth and focus on feel, as you also notice where the club head brushes the ground (bottoms out).

Now you are ready for the third step of the Damage Control pre-shot routine: making a full-speed "preview" swing and checking your divot to verify ball position.

7.2.4 Damage Control Pre-Shot Routine Step 3: Preview Swing/Divot Check

Now make a "preview" swing. This is a full speed practice swing previewing the exact feel and balance of the real swing you are about to make, from just 5-inches away. If you like this swing, and are willing to play the shot with it, look down (before you move your feet) and examine the exact position of where your divot occurred.

Does this divot equal clean ball contact? As you move in to address your ball for your real swing, adjust your ball position to be perfect, centering it exactly where the start of your divot will be (assuming you'll make the same swing, Figure 7.2.4.1).

If your preview swing is not going to make a visible divot, you can still notice where your club starts to brush the grass (or whatever the ball is sitting in). Always make sure your ball is positioned to be hit first, before anything else of significance is encountered by your club head.

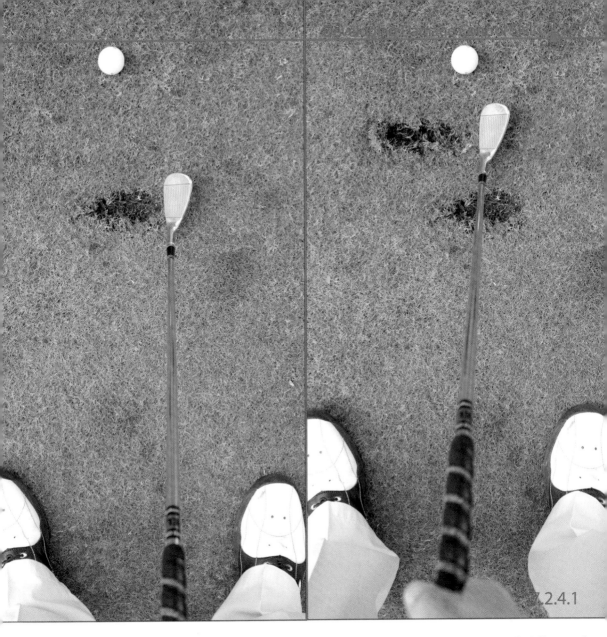

7.2.4.1

This is key: verify the location of where your divot **will start** in your last, good, full-speed practice swing. Then position your body so the ball will be centered on that spot in your real swing. The divot location should be the same for both your preview and real swings. Using your preview swing divot to determine the adjustment in ball position needed as you move in and address the ball, its easy to get the ball in perfect position for your real swing, no matter what slope, stance, or swing obstacles you face.

In the Case of No Space

The Damage Control pre-shot routine must change when there is only enough room to swing while standing over the ball:

A second version of the pre-shot routine must be used when obstacles restrict any swings other than from exactly the same position you need to play from. In this case follow the exact same stutter-step and preview swing concept, except execute all four swings from your real address position over the real ball. No other swing position would accurately duplicate the swing restrictions you are about to encounter. You must be careful not to move the ball or break any branches in any of these swings, and it is impossible to make real speed swings under such conditions. In these cases, make slow-motion backswings and follow-throughs as realistically as possible, even if they must be made separately. Remember, the purpose of the pre-shot routine is to show your brain what you want to do, and how it will feel, before you have to try it for real.

This makes the real thing just a repeat of something you already know how to do, in fact something you've already essentially done!

When a Damage Control pre-shot routine is successful, it provides the feel of the swing you can make in the space available, the balance you'll need, and the perfect ball position. Then with confidence you can duplicate the preview swing and execute the successful escape shot you have planned.

Use this pre-shot routine during your practice, so it becomes a habit as you're learning the skills of Damage Control. When it becomes familiar and natural to you, and you repeat it before trouble shots on the course, it will make executing trouble shots easier and more successful.

7.3 Take it to Your Backyard

ALERT! Damage Control practice sessions consist of sloping surfaces, obstacles, unusual body positions, and intense club resistance/impacts. The materials we've mentioned have been chosen and tested with safety as a priority, but perform all Damage Control drills only at your own risk. Each individual has their own unique physical problems, so consider your own specific limitations and proceed cautiously. Take it slowly. Stretch and warm-up before any practice session, and be careful not to injure your back. Don't hit into anything hard, brittle or dangerous.

Damage Control is a new concept, involving new postures, positions and skills you have never practiced before. Don't over-do it. Proceed wisely and at your own risk.

7.3.1 First let me give you some general drill reminders:

1) **Don't worry about making bad swings** - your bad swings and learning errors don't ruin any scores in your backyard.

2) **Pay attention to your shot patterns** - learn about your scatter directions, not the distances; real balls on the course will give you different distance and size patterns, but they will be similar to the shot pattern shape of the Damage Control balls. Hit groups of 10 shots at a time. Pay special attention to the shot pattern created by your first group of 10 vs. your second group of 10. Usually the first is your worst. Improvement will come with repetition and familiarity.

3) **Pay attention to ball flight** - pay particular attention to your ball launch characteristics, ball flight starting direction and the in-flight curvature of your shots after impact. NOTE - Wind has an exaggerated effect on Damage Control balls compared to real balls, because they are so light. Therefore, the feedback they provide will not be good in windy conditions.

4) **Always observe safety** - Damage Control balls do sting when they hit people, so don't hit them at others. **BE VERY CAREFUL STEPPING ON AND FROM THE PLATFORM WHEN IT IS SLOPED.**

5) **Have fun** - Remember, you are not initially keeping score and you don't have to hit a Damage Control shot perfectly for it to be successful. Each drill should be approached in a relaxed fashion and with a sense of adventure. You will be attempting shots you may have rarely encountered and the resultant penalties in your backyard are nil. These drills have not only been created for your instruction but also your enjoyment. Enjoy and swing away!

7.3.2 Index: Drills vs. Skills

Hand-Fire Feel Drills

2) TAKE IT TO THE COURSE

 Red-Flag Touch Drills

2) TAKE IT TO YOUR GAME

 Damage Control Mentality Drills

7.3.3 Backyard Drills

<u>Drill #1 - Obstacles off Heel of Club</u> (ref. pages: 67+,76,111)

Materials needed: Damage Control balls, foam rock

Step #1)   Take normal address position and feel how you would shank the ball or hit the obstacle

Step #2)   Start pre-shot routine using spine angle set-up-ology, crowd into the ball (move closer to it at address), bend over at the waist, and grip down on your club.

Step #3)   Complete routine to feel the uprightness and reduced power of this set-up

Step #4)   Execute 10 shots and observe resultant shot pattern.

Points of emphasis: 1) Create a more upright swing plane
2) The swing power is reduced because you must grip down on the club
3) You should still be able to take a full swing

Bad   Good

<u>Drill #2 - Obstacles off Toe of Club</u> (ref. pages: 111,113)

Materials needed: Damage Control balls, foam rock

Step #1) Take normal address position and feel how normal impact might hit the obstacle (bottom left photo).

Step #2) Start pre-shot routine using normal set-up-ology except set-up slightly further away from obstacle, playing ball off toe of club

Step #3) Complete routine and imagine reduced power of shot

Step #4) Execute 10 shots and observe the resultant shot pattern.

Points of emphasis: 1) Expect a 25% loss in power
2) Try opened and closed-face swings to gain confidence in swinging close to an object as well as understanding varying shot curvatures.

Bad

Drill #3 - Obstacles in Front of Ball (ref. pages: 78+,109+)

Materials needed: platform, Damage Control balls, foam rock

Step #1) Take normal address position, feel how follow through would hit rock

Step #2) Start pre-shot routine using spine lean set-up-ology, play ball back in stance, lean forward

Step #3) Feel reduced power of this set-up, how the ground will stop club before hitting rock.

Step #4) Execute 10 shots and observe the resultant shot pattern.

Points of emphasis: 1) Use extra lofted on your club
2) Open the clubface to provide an extra margin of loft
3) Aim left of your target and release your grip pressure as you reach impact.

Drill #4 - Obstacles Close Behind Ball (ref. pages: 94+,107)

Materials needed: platform (standing on end in "V" shape), Damage Control balls

Step #1)   Take normal address position, feel how you would have no back swing
Step #2)   Start pre-shot routine using normal set-up-ology, except facing the
                platform with a closed clubface, set ball more toward toe of club than
                normal
Step #3)   Complete routine to feel a normal swing parallel to platform
Step #4)   Execute 10 shots hitting the ball off toe of the club and observe
                low shot trajectories and shot pattern.

Points of emphasis: 1) Use a club with lots of extra loft
                          2) Shots will roll a long way because of zero backspin
                          3) Visualize a trajectory to the left and to the left

<u>Drill #5 - Obstacles Ahead of You</u> (restricted follow through, ref. pgs: 108)

Materials needed: platform, Damage Control balls, foam tree

Step #1)   Take normal address position, feel how you would hit the limb with a full follow-through

Step #2)   Start pre-shot routine using normal set-up-ology

Step #3)   Complete routine to find (and feel) limit of follow through

Step #4)   Execute 10 shots and observe the resultant shot pattern.

Points of emphasis: 1) Try different heights of tree limb
2) Try different distances from limb
3) Learn how much extra room you require on the follow through because stopping the club is always harder than you expect

Drill #6 - Obstacle about 33" Behind Ball (ref. pages: 105+)

Materials needed: platform, Damage Control balls, foam tree

Step #1)   Take normal address position, feel how you hit tree limb with normal backswing.

Step #2)   Start pre-shot routine using normal set-up-ology

Step #3)   Before initiating backswing, pre-cock wrists fully. Then move through 9 position stutter-step swing. Verify club clearance in all positions, including mid-backswing and down swing

Step #4)   Execute 10 shots and observe the resultant shot pattern.

Points of emphasis: 1) Try it first with a wedge, then a 7-iron, then a 4-iron
2) This swing will become more comfortable over time
3) Backswing radius varies with golfer physique, club length and terrain; try this shot from several different slopes

Pre-cock   Back Swing Positions

Down Swing

Through Swing

Drill #7 - Obstacle about 36" Behind the Ball (ref. pages: 104)

Materials needed: platform, Damage Control balls, foam tree

Step #1) Take normal address position, feel how normal backswing hits tree limb

Step #2) Start pre-shot routine using normal set-up-ology, grip down on the club shaft

Step #3) Complete routine to verify swing clearance

Step #4) Execute 10 shots and observe the resultant shot pattern.

Points of emphasis: 1) Any club you shorten will produce less carry distance than normal

2) Your swing arc will be a slightly smaller radius than normal

Drill #8 - Obstacle 38" Behind Ball (ref. pages: 78+,102+)

Materials needed: platform, Damage Control balls, foam tree

Step #1)   Take normal address position, feel how you hit tree limb with normal backswing

Step #2)   Start pre-shot routine using spine lean set-up-ology, lean forward play ball back in stance

Step #3)   Complete routine to feel the swing clearance and balance requirements of swing

Step #4)   Execute 10 shots and observe the resultant shot pattern.

Points of emphasis: 1) Your club will have less effective loft
2) The shot will fly lower than normal
3) Your swing radius (of clubhead) will be normal, so distance will still be strong

Drill #9 - Obstacles Above your Head (requiring flat swings, ref. ps: 71,77,125)

Materials needed: platform, Damage Control balls, foam tree

Step #1)   Take normal address position, feel how you would hit the tree limb in your backswing.

Step #2)   Start pre-shot routine using spine (trunk) angle set-up-ology, squatting down at address

Step #3)   Complete routine to feel how low you need to squat (or kneel) for swing clearance

Step #4)   Execute 10 shots and observe the resultant shot pattern.

Points of emphasis:

1) It is more difficult to rotate when squatting, so power will be limited

2) The lower the limb the flatter your swing plane must be

3) Lower limb height until it forces you onto your knees. You'll be surprised at the power you can still generate.

Drill #10 - Backswing Limitations requiring Upright Swing Planes
(ref. pages: 69+,126)

Materials needed: Damage Control balls, foam tree

Step #1)	Take normal address position, feel how you would hit the tree in your normal swing plane.
Step #2)	Start pre-shot routine using spine angle set-up-ology, move closer to ball, bend over more, grip down on club (or use shorter club)
Step #3)	Complete routine to feel surprisingly powerful shoulder turn
Step #4)	Execute 10 shots and observe the resultant shot pattern.

Points of emphasis: 1) The more you bend over the more upright the swing plane
2) You will need to use a shorter club when you bend over.

Bad   Good

Drill #11 - Ball sitting up Above Ground (ref. pages: 75,132+)

Materials needed: platform (standing in inverted-V shape), Damage Control balls, foam rock, long tee

Step #1)   Start pre-shot routine using spine angle (standing vertical) set-up-ology with club 3 inches above ball

Step #2)   Complete routine to feel how heavy club feels during swing

Step #3)   Execute 10 shots and observe the resultant shot pattern.

Points of emphasis: 1) Try hitting shots at different heights to see effect of club loft directing the ball to left instead of up

2) The more horizontal your swing and farther away from your body the ball is, the heavier your club will feel.

3) A heavier club feel increases your tendency to hit below (under) the ball

4) The higher the ball, the flatter your swing and more vertical your spine needs to be

Drill #12 - Fading Shots around Obstacles (ex. tree) (ref. pages: 94+,138+)

Materials needed:platform, Damage Control balls, foam tree

Step #1)   Take normal address position, feel how you would hit the tree with a normal shot trajectory

Step #2)   Start pre-shot routine using normal set-up-ology, aim two steps left of tree and open the clubface slightly.

Step #3)   Complete routine to visualize swinging along the set-up line, and the ball fading around tree

Step #4)   Execute 10 shots and observe the resultant shot pattern.

Points of emphasis: 1) Start with short shots and slow swing speeds
2) As tempo and distances are increased, notice the shots start on the same line, but the curve increases
3) Opening the club face starts shot farther right, curves them more, and launches them higher with more backspin

Drill #13 - Drawing Ball Around Obstacle (ref. pages: 94+,138+,143))

Materials needed: : platform, Damage Control balls, foam tree

Step #1)   Take normal address position, feel how you would hit the tree with a normal shot trajectory

Step #2)   Start pre-shot routine using normal set-up-ology except aim two steps right of tree and close the clubface slightly.

Step #3)   Complete routine, visualize ball drawing around tree

Step #4)   Execute 10 shots and observe the resultant shot pattern.

Points of emphasis: 1) Start with short shots (slow swing speeds), gradually increase swing tempo (notice shots start on same line, but curve more)
2) Try aiming farther right, closing clubface more
3) Visualize shot trajectory prior to shot execution (focus on learning how closing clubface starts shot farther left, creates more hook, lower trajectory, less spin)

Drill #14 - Sidehill Terrain ... Ball Above Feet (ref. pages: 64,130+)

Materials needed: platform, cinder blocks supporting under hinge), Damage Control balls

Step #1)   Take normal address position, feel club is too long, club face aims left

Step #2)   Start pre-shot routine using spine angle set-up-ology (stand more vertical), grip down on club, aim right of target

Step #3)   Complete routine to feel normal hand (non-blocking) action

Step #4)   Execute 10 shots and observe the resultant shot pattern.

Points of emphasis: 1) Start with 1/2 swing, repeat 10-shot sessions with a full swing.
2) Try sessions with different slope heights
3) Try sessions with different club lofts
4) Learn correlation: the greater the slope and club loft, the more right you must aim

Drill #15 - Sidehill Terrain … Ball Below Feet (ref. pages: 64,73,134)

Materials needed: platform, cinder blocks support under hinge, Damage Control balls

Step #1) Take normal address position, feel club is too short
Step #2) Start pre-shot routine using spine angle set-up-ology, retain normal spine angle to ground, squat down to reach ball
Step #3) Complete routine to feel limited rotation and strain on balance
Step #4) Execute 10 shots and observe the resultant shot pattern.

Points of emphasis: 1) Heel of club hits platform, toe does not
2) Try different slopes, different shot distances
3) Aim directly at target (notice clubface does not aim right of target)

Drill #16 - Downhill Terrain ... Front Foot Below Back (ref. pages: 80+,85,135)

Materials needed: platform, cinder blocks support under hinge, Damage Control balls

Step #1) Take normal address position (vertical spine); feel how swing and club bottom-out behind ball, would hit shot fat

Step #2) Start pre-shot routine using spine lean and stance width set-up-ology, play ball back in stance, lean forward to get spine perpendicular to slope, widen stance for balance

Step #3) Complete routine to feel limited body rotation, pressure on leading leg, imbalance on follow through, verify divot location

Step #4) Execute 10 shots and observe the resultant shot pattern.

Points of emphasis: 1) Decreased effective loft and lower launch angle will make ball bounce and roll farther than normal, especially on shorter shots
2) Learning exact divot location for ball position is paramount
3) Complete swing past impact before walking-through to catch balance

Drill #17 - Uphill Terrain ... Front Foot Above Back (ref. pages: 82+,136+)

Materials needed: : platform, cinder blocks support under hinge, Damage Control balls

Step #1)   Take normal address position, feel club would dig into ground after impact, might hurt wrist

Step #2)   Start pre-shot routine using spine lean and stance width set-up-ology, lean forward, get spine perpendicular to slope, widen stance for balance

Step #3)   Complete Routine to feel gravity fighting rotation through impact, pressure on back leg, fall-back imbalance on follow through

Step #4)   Execute 10 shots and observe the resultant shot pattern.

Points of emphasis: 1) Notice increased effective loft launches shots higher, promotes leaving shots short of target (use less lofted club to compensate)
2) Focus on turning-through impact, before stepping-back after impact to catch balance

Drill #18 - Back-Hand Swing (ref. pages: 128)

Materials needed: platform, foam tree, Damage Control balls

Step #1)   Start pre-shot routine with backhand set-up-ology
         -Play ball about 3 inches out in front of toe line
         -Put free hand on shoulder (to anchor pivot point during swing)
         -Keep clubface perpendicular to target line
Step #2)   Complete Routine feel surprising power, verify divot location
Step #3)   Move in and execute 10 shots, observe the shot pattern

Points of emphasis: 1) Grip club with arm hanging straight down shoulder
         2) Place finger on shaft for added control of clubface
         3) Experiment with different clubs (for loft and distance changes)

Drill #19 - Opposite Way Swings (ref. pages: 129)

Materials needed: : platform, foam tree, Damage Control balls

Step #1)   Start pre-shot routine with normal set-up-ology except take grip opposite from normal grip, turn 5-iron upside down (toe down)

Step #2)   Complete preview swing with feel of smooth, accelerating motion

Step #3)   Focus on repeating preview swing motion and feel to make solid contact with ball

Step #4)   Move in and execute 10 shots, observe the shot pattern

Points of emphasis: 1) Take special notice of club loft vs. shot height and direction
2) Opposite way swings require many repetitions to eliminate feel of awkwardness
3) Try different clubs to find optimum trajectory for distance, then find optimum club to produce lofted shots

<u>Hand-Fire Feel warm-ups - 1) **Dead Hands**</u> (ref. pages: 160)

Steps: 1) Use grip pressure = 0; hand action = 0; brute force = 0
2) Swing 10 times without, 10 times with Damage Control ball
3) Learn feel of how lightly you can grip club and swing without slippage

<u>Hand-Fire Feel warm-ups - 2) **Wrist Cock vs. Wrist Hinge**</u> (ref. pages: 156+,165,170)

(Separate good feel of wrist cock from bad feel of wrist hinge (break down))

Steps: 1) Gradually cock wrists to full cock at top of backswing
2) Swing through impact zone with smooth acceleration, to full cock at finish
3) Repeat swing motion with eyes closed to feel wrist cock as isolated movement
4) Now try hinging wrists to verify feel of what NOT to do.

Hand-Fire Feel warm-ups - 3) Forearm Rotation (ref. pages: 157,162+,171)

Steps: 1) Swing 10 times with, 10 without a Damage Control ball, over exaggerate the rolling over of forearms

2) Hit shots slowing down, then speeding up forearm rotation

3) Learn how forearm rotation tempo is critical to ball curvature: impact with clubface open causes slice, clubface closed causes hook

Hand-Fire Feel warm-ups - 4) Brute Force (ref. pages: 166+,172+,180+)

Steps: 1) Set club at one edge of open doorway (as if it were a ball; you can also try to lift cement blocks as shown)

2) Exert light pressure to feel beginnings of brute force in forearms and wrists

3) Exert more pressure to feel demands in arms and shoulders; ultimately with maximum force, feel brute force through chest, legs, even toes

Drill #20 - A Little Smoke for Fried-Egg Lie (ref. pages: 174+)

Materials needed: tray, sand, Damage Control balls

Step #1)   In 2" deep sand in tray, swirl ball in circles to create fried-egg lie
Step #2)   Start pre-shot routine with normal bunker set-up-ology
Step #3)   Complete preview swing (above ball) feeling more hand fire than normal
Step #4)   Move in and execute 10 shots, observe the shot pattern

Points of emphasis:

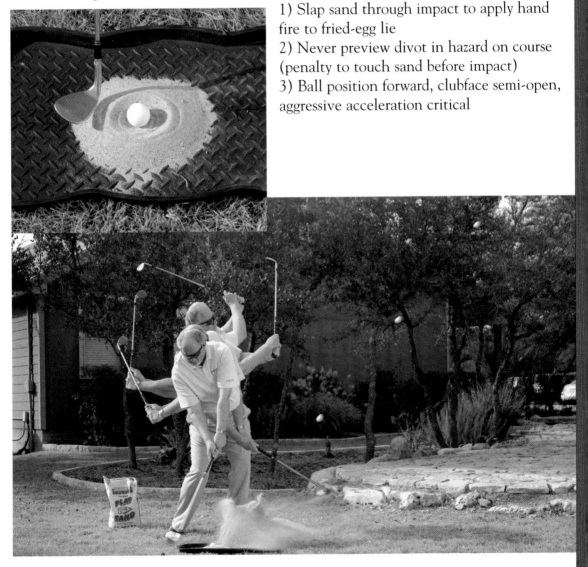

1) Slap sand through impact to apply hand fire to fried-egg lie
2) Never preview divot in hazard on course (penalty to touch sand before impact)
3) Ball position forward, clubface semi-open, aggressive acceleration critical

Drill #21 - Smoldering to Open Flames for Wet Sand (ref. pages: 177+)

Materials needed: tray, sand, water, bucket, Damage Control balls

Step #1)   Wet sand in bucket, pile wet sand 3" deep in tray, create buried lie
Step #2)   Start pre-shot routine with set-up-ology (position ball 1" forward of stance center, close club face)
Step #3)   Complete preview swing with feel for applying brute force through impact
Step #4)   Move in and execute 10 shots, observe the shot pattern

Points of emphasis:

1) Ample hand, forearm, wrist strength required to prevent wrist breakdown after impact

2) Learn correlation of shot length proportional to follow through (long follow through = long shot, short follow through = short shot)

3) Shot carry distance shorter, trajectory lower than normal

4) Expect zero backspin (long roll-out) on green

Drill #22 - Blast Furnace from Packed Mud or Water (ref. pages: 166+,172+,180+)

Materials needed: tray, sand, cedar mulch, bucket, water, Damage Control balls

Step #1)   Wet/mix sand, mulch, water in bucket, pile 4" deep, create buried lie
Step #2)   Start pre-shot routine with set-up-ology (ball position center of stance, club face toed in)
Step #3)   Complete preview swing prepared to supply maximum hand-fire
Step #4)   Move in and execute 10 shots, observe the shot pattern

Points of emphasis:
1) 1) BE CAREFUL: This shot requires strength. There is potential for injury. Approach shot wisely. If you doubt getting ball out when on course, take unplayable lie

7.3.4 Double-up, triple-up, a combination of all problems!

In this chapter we've addressed a number of problems you will encounter on the golf course, and how to practice them in your backyard. To experience and develop all the swings suggested will take you a number of practice sessions. If you do them the results will be fundamental and meaningful to your game. Having said this however, there is an additional and elevated level of Damage Control you can achieve in your game..

Additional competence (and still lower scores) will come from developing the ability to hit shots from trouble lies which involve multiple difficulty factors. You've seen how we recommend handling a lie behind a rock, under a tree limb or on a down slope. Now imagine how to hit a shot with the ball above your feet, a tree in your back swing (Figure 7.3.4.1) and maybe a large rock in front of the ball, all at the same time.

I'm sure you'll realize how difficult that shot would be, and if you think about it, how the shots and skills of Damage Control are virtually endless. You can practice as many combinations of problems as you like in your own backyard, but you'll never exhaust all the possibilities. You can set your platform high or low at any angle, move your phony tree limbs or rocks to any position, and lean or tilt your spine to as many angles as you can imagine. You will still not encounter a swing that some golfer hasn't needed on a golf course somewhere before, or might need in the future.

7.3.4.1

7.3.5 Backyard Fun

We've detailed lots of new concepts, shots, skills, and backyard practice drills so far, and I know they can help you improve your game consistently. But I want to make another point of emphasis however, which doesn't relate to scoring: – KEEP IT FUN!

Keep your backyard practice sessions fun by hitting funky shots from funky lies, and try miracle escape shots – all with your Damage Control balls. How high can you loft shots? How low can you go? See and stretch your golf skill boundaries. And have fun while you learn. The more fun it is, the more you'll do it, and the more it will help your game!

Friendly competition is the best way to stay focused during practice sessions – because it makes you try harder to hit every shot better to win the game. Play games with your family, your kids or friends. Create difficult lie conditions, pick targets, and the closest to the target wins the point!

7.3.5.1

7.4 Take it to the Course

At this point it's time for a quick status check. Earlier you've seen how to set up a practice facility and develop the skills of Set-up-ology, Swing Shaping, and Hand-Fire Feel at home in your backyard. Let's assume you're going to do the drills we've suggested, and learn to make the swings and hit reasonable shots from those circumstances. In fact, let's assume you're going to get really good at the first three skills of Damage Control.

Then it will be time to play Damage Control practice-rounds with real balls, to real targets, to "take it to the course". Once you've learned to make the swings and hit shots from trouble, you need to learn where those shots are going to fly, and how they're going to react once they get there. That is: you need to learn your shot-patterns and you need some Red-Flag touch.

7.4.1 Find Trouble on your Course and Play From It

The Damage Control practice round is a really fun round to play. There is no score keeping involved, no specified number of holes or shots you hit, and no "rules of play". Sound like fun? You bet it is!

The point of the round is to locate trouble you normally get into on your course, all 18-holes, and learn to play from it. I recommend doing this in early mornings or late evenings, when the course is relatively empty (so you won't bother those trying to keep serious score). Here's how a Damage Control practice round is played.

Go to the first tee but don't hit a shot. Look out and identify the trouble you normally drive into. Then drive your cart straight there and throw 10 balls into it. Make sure all the balls are in some kind of trouble, choose a target, and hit all 10 according to the Damage Control principles you've been learning in your backyard. Then look at your shot-pattern and soak in some knowledge.

This is a snapshot of what your shot-pattern looks like from this trouble. It's only 10 shots, so it's not your ultimate shot-pattern. It's a quick look, an initial indication, a first idea of what your shot-pattern really looks like from here. It's not the final answer but it's a start towards one.

Just look at it, then pick up your balls and move on. Don't get hung up on the accuracy or inaccuracy of anything here. Just pick up the 10 balls, get in your cart, drive to the

worst trouble you can find around the first green, and throw your 10 balls into it. Then repeat your "escape-from-trouble" scenario again: choose a target; hit 10 trouble shots; observe your shot-pattern; pick up your balls and move to the next hole.

Move around the course in your Damage Control practice round, all 18-holes, devoting your entire attention to finding and playing Damage Control shots. (Note: make sure you don't hold up any play). You're looking for (evaluating) trouble: high grass, sand with deep lips, severe slopes, water edges, steep banks, shots from the rough on slopes over water (Figure 7.4.1.1), low hanging tree limbs, or fences. Consider anything that's given you trouble in the past or you think may do so in the future.

Remember; no scoring, no putting out, no normal game shots; just relax and have fun. This is a Damage Control practice round; you're looking at shot-patterns and watching how shots behave with little or no backspin, to develop your Red-Flag touch. A nice thing is you're also refining your Damage Control Set-up-ology, Swing Shaping and Hand-Fire Feel at the same time!

7.4.2 Establish "quick-view" shot-patterns

After you play 10-shots to establish a "quick-view" escape shot-pattern, look at it but don't stress over it. Respect it because it has meaning. If your pattern is poor, recognize that and make a mental note to practice this lie in your next backyard session. But don't stay there all day hitting shots until you get them to be perfect. Don't overanalyze or treat

any particular trouble area as being overly important. Remember, there are an infinite number of them, and you only hit 10 shots from that particular one.

The primary objective is to train your brain to imagine where your trouble shots are most likely to go. If you could hit a million shots from every trouble lie imaginable, your Damage Controller would know what your shot-pattern is in each case. But 10 shots at a time will give you an idea (Figure 7.4.2.1).

Exercise your brain. Teach it to imagine. Project an image in your mind's eye, then hit 10 shots and see the result. Compare your estimate with reality. Learn, study, grow, and stretch: this is the way poor players become better and good players become great. Prepare yourself for the situations you expect to get into, and the results you expect to see getting out. As you develop the skills of shot-pattern recognition and Red-Flag touch, you'll find the rest of your Damage Control skills coalescing and improving, and your confidence from trouble situations will soar.

7.4.3 Do NOT keep score

While practicing funky shots from funky lies, try miracle escape shots. Use old balls for the really dangerous shots that don't have much chance of success. Have fun while you learn. Before you hit the shot, imagine the shot trajectory and how the ball will react after it lands. Then execute and watch; is it what you expected? It's OK to try shots that aren't likely to succeed, because knowing the reality of your chances will help your target selection in the future.

Again I remind you: don't hold up play. I don't want to get you (or me) into trouble with your golf professional, fellow members or the course ranger. Other golfers might either think you're crazy, or be irritated by your practice on the course. Many have been told to practice only in designated areas, never on the course. But you can't practice Damage Control on perfectly flat driving range tees, or from perfect fairway lies. You must do it from real trouble on the course.

One more favor I ask. When you're practicing Damage Control on course, please fix every pitch-mark you make on a green. If you're practicing from a grassy creek bank and happened to fly eight of 10 shots onto the green, please fix all eight of those marks. Your fellow members will appreciate your efforts, the condition of your greens and your putting will benefit, and you'll be much less likely to get in trouble for your Damage Control practice.

7.4.4 Pick your "top-three"

In your third Damage Control round , pick the three "most-likely" lies to cause you trouble on the entire course, and hit 25 escape shots (instead of 10) from each. Do this evaluation by looking at every hole for its maximum trouble, combined with the way you tend to miss shots (Figure 7.4.4.1). If your bad shots are slices to the right, pay special attention to trouble on the right. This evaluation will give you a better look at your true shot-pattern size, and help you be better prepared for the trouble you're most likely to face on your next round.

7.4.5 Focus on Red-Flag touch

Be sure to pick some trouble spots near true Red-Flag landing areas, because launching good escape shots from trouble is only the first part of the equation. When a well struck escape shot lands on the downhill slope of a firm green and rolls over into water, you still have to count the disaster score. It doesn't matter that you executed a good swing and played the shot exactly the way you wanted (Figure 7.4.5.1).

The best way to train your Red-Flag when to stand up, is to see enough well-struck shots end up perfectly, while others end up in trouble. Then learn what caused the difference. Don't hesitate to find extremely difficult trouble spots, and hit shots from them repeatedly, even if your shots turn out disastrously. From this kind of practice, you'll find there is usually a statistically best play. Often it won't be a 100% solution, but if it's the best solution for a given situation, you need to know what it is. That's the one you want to play from that spot in a tournament.

There are at least a few Red-Flag landing areas on essentially every course, and you need to learn to deal with the ones that affect your scores most often. You should also realize there are areas on courses around the world with much more severe and disastrous consequences than those you play from. And it's important to note, the penalties for misjudgments in Red-Flag touch are magnified as greens get firmer and faster. For this reason you should play at least a couple of Damage Control rounds every year, to keep your Red-Flag touch sharp (because greens are getting faster every year, and there is always room to improve your touch)

And don't worry about getting "too-good" at this. As you become a better player, you can always find courses which present more difficult challenges to keep things interesting.

7.5 Take it to Your Game

After you've played several Damage Control practice rounds, you need to go back to playing normal golf. When you do, having learned to set up, shape your swings, use your hands, estimate shot-patterns and recognize Red-Flag areas when you find yourself in trouble, your game will be better. You'll avoid most disasters, and shoot somewhat lower scores right off the bat.

There is still one final step you can take however, to optimize the effect of Damage Control on your game. That is to optimize the part of your Damage Control mentality that makes shot choices and target selections, so they optimally fit with the talent and skill level of the rest of your game. We suggest doing this by playing two very special Damage Control rounds on two consecutive days (so the state of your game will be reasonably constant for both rounds).

7.5.1 Play an over-the-top "Supergamble" Damage Control round

Some golfers hesitate to devote a round of golf to an experiment, because the round might otherwise be the best round of their life. Knowing how remote the chance of this is, I suggest you devote two special rounds for the express purpose of optimizing your Damage Control mentality. The chance of you then having a career best round will dramatically improve.

The first experimental round should be played with your Damage Control attitude set at the "extremely aggressive" end of the decision spectrum. We call this an over-the-top Supergamble Damage Control round. It means on every shot you play with the flagstick as your target. No matter what's in your way, no matter how close a creek or a tree limb or out of bounds stake, you go for the flag.

This round takes no extra time, no extra effort, you simply need to be focused and aware of the choices you're making on every shot. No matter what trouble you might get into, you fire at the flag all day long. No matter how narrow the fairway, go for it with a driver. Assume you'll hit a perfect shot every time you swing, no matter the consequences if you don't.

That's it, that's all you do in your Supergamble round besides keep score. Don't worry about anything, play as hard as you can, let it fly, and see how you score.

7.5.2 Then Play an over-the-top "Supersafe" Damage Control Round

The next day change your attitude so it's like you're a different player. This day play your over-the-top Damage Control round from the other end of the decision spectrum. Make every decision on every shot with a Supersafe mentality.

Don't try to do anything special or take any chances or gambles. Keep your focus all the way around the course on playing safe (choose all shots to targets at 95% or more safe), just to see and feel the difference from yesterday. Then see how this mentality affects your score.

7.5.3 Balance your Results

I have never yet seen a golfer who played their best when playing every trouble shot Supersafe. Likewise, I have never seen a golfer who played their best while gambling to the max every time. Everyone has a balance point in their aggression scale which will be best for their overall scoring capability, and it always lies somewhere between the completely safe (zero% gamble) and full-out 100% gamble ends of the spectrum.

Where this balance point is for any particular golfer depends on their Damage Control skills. It can also change as the situation or need for a particular result changes. Although its all still new to us, from the results we've seen so far this balance point doesn't change nearly as much as golfers expect it to.

The point of devoting two special rounds to using extreme Damage Control mentality is to see where the limits of aggression vs. safety take your game. As you analyze these two rounds after completion, you can begin to move toward striking a balance within your own game as to how aggressively you should play to score your best. Did you waste a few strokes when you were playing too safe? You probably did. Did you waste several strokes by playing to aggressively? Again, you probably did.

For every golfer there is an optimum amount of aggression they should use in choosing targets from trouble lies. If you're a numbers person, you'll want to put a number on how aggressively you should play. For others a number will bother them, and they'll be better off just feeling how aggressively they should play.

For me personally, I've settled on a low aggression level, preferring to play to targets I believe safe in the 80 to 90% range. I came to this after watching how the best players in the world escape and recover from trouble, while amateurs of all skill levels in my schools struggle violently with disaster scores and disaster holes. When I play from trouble at this level, I hit my best shots and my short game allows me to score my best.

You must base your aggression level on the state of your five physical and mental skills of Damage Control, with consideration given to how strong your short game and putting are. Are they at least good enough to save strokes when in a position to do so?

7.5.4 Go Lower Your Scores

So there you have it, our concept of Damage Control: Five skills to help you avoid disaster scores and disaster holes. You can learn the three skills of Set-up-ology, Swing Shaping and Hand-Fire Feel in your backyard. You can play Damage Control practice-rounds and refine those three skills while you learn what your shot-patterns look like, and develop your Red-Flag Touch. Then you can play special rounds of normal golf with your attention focused on optimizing your Damage Control Mentality.

Obviously you can work in your backyard as often as you want. It will probably take you several Damage Control practice rounds to get a good feel for your shot-patterns and Red-Flag Touch. And within a few months of normal play you should feel you're honing in on an optimum Damage Control mentality for your game and skill level.

Your scores should improve gradually during this entire time, and once you begin playing with an aggression level that befits your game, your scores will have dropped consistently to a new level. That's our goal ... I hope you'll make it yours.

Another thing. While you watch PGA or LPGA Tour pros on television, observe how they play (and execute) shots from trouble. With your attention on optimizing your own Damage Control game, you can learn a few tricks of the trade. And one last thought: as you practice and develop your own version of Damage Control practice in your backyard, send us photos of the learning aids you develop and the on-course trouble you find.

The concept of Damage Control is new and we don't have all the answers. I'm sure we have much to learn. Visit our website (www.pelzgolf.com) for the latest in Damage Control developments from our research and your feedback.

Thanks in advance, and I hope as you work on your Damage Control skills, you see lower scores as a reward.

Good luck, and lower scores to you,

Dave Pelz

Photo Credit List

Grateful acknowledgement is made to the following photographers and organizations for permission to reproduce their work:

Leonard Kamsler: Back cover, Pgs. 25, 48, 49, 59AB, 60, 64AB, 65, 73B, 81C, 87AB, 105AB, 121C, 128ABCDE, 129AB, 130, 134A, 136, 140ABC, 151, 152, 153A, 158, 159ABCDEF, 161ABC, 162ABC, 163, 164B, 165, 177, 178ABCD, 179, 180A, 181, 182ABC, 185, 186, 187, 194, 197, 200, 201, 207, 208, 213, 217, 244, 259A.

Pelz Golf Institute by Joel Mendelman: Cover, front matter pg. 4, Pgs. 2, 3, 22, 27AB, 28AB, 29, 31AB, 34AB, 35AB, 36, 37, 38, 43, 44, 45, 54, 55, 57, 58, 61, 62, 63, 68ABC, 69, 70, 71AB, 72, 73A, 74, 75ABC, 76AB, 77ABC, 78AB, 79AB, 80, 81AB, 82, 83, 85ABC, 89ABCDEF, 91ABCDEF, 93, 95ABCDEF, 96, 97, 99, 100, 101, 103ABCD, 104AB, 106ABCD, 107ABC, 108ABC, 109, 110AB, 111ABCDEF, 118, 121A, 122, 123, 124, 125, 126AB, 127, 131AB, 132B, 133, 134B, 135, 137, 142, 143, 147, 148, 149, 153B, 156, 157AB, 160, 167ABC, 168, 170AB, 171AB, 172, 173AB, 175, 176AB, 189, 191ABC, 218, 219, 220, 223, 224, 226, 227AB, 228, 229AB, 230AB, 231AB, 232AB, 237, 247, 248, 250, 256, 257, 259B, 260, 262, 263ABC, 265ABCDEFGHI, 267AB, 272ABCD, 273ABC, 274ABC, 275ABC, 276, 277ABC, 278, 279AB, 280AB, 281AB, 282, 283AB, 284AB, 285, 286AB, 287AB, 288AB, 289AB, 290AB, 291ABC, 292AB, 293AB, 294AB, 295AB, 296, 297, 299, 300, 301, 302.

Pelz Golf Institute by Eddie Pelz: Pgs. 12, 121B, 154, 195, 209AB, 225.

The Golf Channel: Pgs. 164A, 205.

AP Photo: Pgs. 21A – Jeff Roberson; 24A and B – Lenny Ignelzi; 132A – Ted S. Warren; 180B – Ann Heisenfelt.

Wire Image: Pgs. 21C – Hunter Martin; 23 – Pete Fontaine; 155 – Sam Greenwood; 183 – Action Images; 198 - Christopher Condon; 199 - Action Images; 203 – Charles Briscoe-Knight.

Getty Images: Pgs. 21B – Andrew Redington; 24C – David Cannon.